WHEN YOU SEE IT

Advance Praise for *When You See It*

"Millions have seen the story on television about the man who became famous in death as *Dirty John*. The end of that story is as well documented as it is dramatic. This story, Tonia Bales's story, fascinating and instructive, is about its beginnings. It is raw and real as Tonia takes the reader into what became a truly harrowing world, and then through it to a new understanding. Characters like Dirty John show up here and there and everywhere. Not often, perhaps, but often enough to make Tonia Bales required reading."

—Keith Morrison, *Dateline NBC*

HOW I OUTSMARTED & OUTLASTED DIRTY JOHN

WHEN YOU SEE IT

TONIA BALES

& AMY JAUMAN

A POST HILL PRESS BOOK
ISBN: 979-8-88845-940-9
ISBN (eBook): 979-8-88845-941-6

When You See It:
How I Outsmarted & Outlasted Dirty John

Cover design by Conroy Accord

This book, as well as any other Post Hill Press publications, may be purchased in bulk quantities at a special discounted rate. Contact orders@posthillpress.com for more information.

This is a work of nonfiction. All people, locations, events, and situations are portrayed to the best of the author's memory and knowledge. Although adequate research was undergone concerning criminal cases, real-life people and perceptions, and authentic situations and incidents, the author and publisher do not assume and hereby disclaim any liability concerning any legal or criminal details present in this book. Some names and identifying details have been changed to protect the privacy of the people involved.

Post Hill Press
New York • Nashville
posthillpress.com

Published in the United States of America
1 2 3 4 5 6 7 8 9 10

For Emily and Abigail, it was always for you.

And for everyone who was just looking for love;
you're not crazy and you're not alone.

TABLE OF CONTENTS

FOREWORD

BY LAURA RICHARDS

In America, four women are murdered by a former or current male partner a day (Rachel Louise Snyder, 2019).

Globally, a woman is murdered every ten minutes by their intimate partner or family member (UN Report, 2024).

The most dangerous place for a woman is in the home (UN Report, 2018).

I first met Tonia in 2018. It was after the hit podcast *Dirty John* had dropped. The Bravo show of the same name—which became a Netflix sensation—was soon to premiere. We met for lunch in a restaurant overlooking the Hollywood Hills. Tonia shared with me that she had been to therapy and that she was glad she had done the work to deal with everything she had gone through with John. I was impressed. Tonia was eloquent and articulate, with a quiet strength, determination, and presence about her.

I forewarned her, however, that she only knew what she knew, and that John Meehan was far more prolific and diabolical than even she suspected. I stated matter-of-factly that a deep-dive reinvestigation was needed—a psychological autopsy—to gain a true understanding of who John Meehan really was and how many people he had harmed. Debra Newell met John toward the end of his life, and by then he was an accomplished manipulator. But questions remained about his childhood: When did he start acting out and harming people? What was really going on in his family relationships, or with Tonia, his first wife of ten years? And what was he up to when he lived away from her?

Tonia bravely agreed to ask the tough questions in our investigative podcast, *The First Wife: John Meehan's Reign of Terror*. Many people spoke out for the first time, including ex-girlfriends, family members, friends, and detectives. Tonia and our team made sense of all this new information in real time. You will learn much more in this book.

It's not been an easy journey for Tonia and her lovely daughters, Emily and Abby. Rather than protect the children from John, the family courts placed them further at risk and enabled his behavior. Currently, serial domestic abusers' and stalkers' histories are not routinely cross-referenced, and just like John, these men have free rein to terrorize multiple victims.

What happened to Tonia could happen to anyone. Psychopaths don't have two heads. They are the men that we date. They are charming, fun, and present as everything you want and need them to be—so much so that many, including those closest to us, also fall for their pathological lies and diabolical ruses. They are extremely manipulative and devious, and they are vengeful when crossed. Many do not survive them.

Tonia did. She is one of the lucky ones. Tonia was determined to protect her children at all costs, and that intense fire, resilience, and power from deep within is the reason she is alive to tell you her story today.

I truly admire Tonia's strength, honesty, and mental fortitude. Sharing her story will help many understand coercive and controlling behavior and how psychopaths operate. Pay attention to the red flags.

Man dies after being stabbed by woman he assaulted with knife, police say

August 25, 2016, *Daily Pilot*

A man stabbed multiple times Saturday evening by a woman who police say he attacked with a knife on the roof of an apartment complex parking structure in Newport Beach has died, authorities said Thursday.

Authorities identified the man as John Michael Meehan, 57, of Cathedral City.

Police said the altercation began at about 5:30 p.m. Saturday when Meehan approached a woman atop the parking structure of the Coronado at Newport apartment complex in the 1900 block of Sherington Place and assaulted her with the knife. Police did not identify the woman but said she is a Newport Beach resident in her 20s.

The woman suffered several lacerations before she grabbed the knife and stabbed Meehan several times, said Newport Beach police spokeswoman Jennifer Manzella.

"There was no verbal altercation that preceded the activity," Manzella said.

Manzella said Meehan and the woman were not related by blood or romantically involved but had "an ongoing troubled relationship."

The woman was treated by paramedics and then taken to a hospital.

Meehan was taken to Orange County Global Medical Center in Santa Ana, where he died of his injuries just after 10 p.m. Wednesday, authorities said.

No arrests were made. Detectives will forward results of their investigation to the Orange County district attorney's office for review, Manzella said.

A NOTE FOR THE READER

The time I spent with John Meehan—the man the world would come to know as "Dirty John"—spans decades. Our story involved multiple police agencies and detectives in several states. It even requires some understanding of laws and how they've changed over time, some knowledge of drug diversion, and the various names of commonly abused medications. Even though there are descriptions of important terms throughout the book, I wanted to provide a resource at the start of the book so that the reader would be able to quickly check a description or definition as needed to best understand the severity of what's happening throughout the book.

I hope you'll refer back to this page as needed and even do your own research on how the important topics of coercive control and drug diversion develop over time.

People

Abby	Tonia and John's youngest daughter
Commander John Burke	Worked with Detective Dennis Luken on the Warren County Drug Task Force (WCDT)
Dan	John's brother, who died of an overdose
Detective Dennis Luken	Detective who investigated John (primarily drug offenses) from 2002 until John's death
Detective Julia Bowman	Detective in Laguna Beach, California, who conducted the investigation into John (primarily stalking offenses) that resulted in his incarceration
Detective Tim Parker	Detective with the Springboro Police Department who worked with Tonia in Ohio from 2000 to 2002
Donna	John's sister, who had the most contact with John over the years
Dr. Bob	Anesthesiologist in Michigan who was a friend of both John and Tonia but later became Tonia's informant
Elaine Jones	Pharmacy board director who worked with the police to investigate John's drug diversion
Ellen	Tonia's attorney
Emily	Tonia and John's oldest daughter

John and Lois Schikner	Tonia's neighbors in Ohio (John Schikner, often called Mr. Schikner, attended most of Tonia's court appearances to offer support)
Jordan	John's biological son
Karen	John's sister
Mark	John's anesthesia school classmate and confidant
Meg	John's girlfriend, who worked with Detective Luken as an informant
Michael	John's younger half-brother
Warren County Drug Task Force (WCDT)	Law enforcement unit focused on combating drug-related crimes and trafficking within Warren County, Ohio

Key Terms

coercive control	A strategic pattern of behavior designed to exploit, control, create dependency, and dominate. The victim's everyday existence is micromanaged and controlled by the abuser.
CPO	A civil protection order (CPO) is a court order that requires an individual to stay away from and have no contact with the party seeking the order.

CRNAs	Certified registered nurse anesthesiologists (CRNAs) are advanced-practice registered nurses who administer anesthesia both autonomously and in collaboration with a variety of health providers. The CRNA cares for patients of all acuity levels in every setting, including but not limited to surgical, obstetrical, diagnostic, therapeutic, and pain management.
data mining	The process of extracting personal information or insights from individuals' answers to questions, with the intent to use that information against them later.
gaslighting	A manipulative technique where a person seeks to make someone doubt their own perception, memory, or reality.
grey rocking	The strategy of disengaging from manipulative or toxic individuals by becoming emotionally distant, unresponsive, and uninteresting, making it difficult for them to provoke a reaction or gain control.
locum tenens	A temporary professional, often in the medical field, who fills in for another employee during their absence or while a position is open.

love bombing	A manipulative tactic where someone overwhelms another with excessive attention, affection, and compliments to gain control or influence over them.
narcissist	An individual with a personality disorder characterized by an excessive sense of self-importance, a need for admiration, and a lack of empathy for others.
psychopath	Individuals with a personality disorder characterized as charming, deeply manipulative, motivated by power and control, who use coercive control, have no moral code, empathy, and are chameleon-esque pathological liars with prefrontal cortex and amygdala brain anomalies.
sociopath	An individual with a personality disorder marked by manipulative and self-focused actions, and while they do not believe the rules apply to them, they do have a moral code and can feel shame; their behaviors are typically a consequence of abuse or childhood trauma.
stalking	Repeated and unwanted attention, harassment, or surveillance of an individual that causes them fear or distress.

TPO	A temporary protective order (TPO) is a court order that provides immediate short-term protection to a person who is experiencing or is at risk of stalking, harassment, or other harm from another person. TPOs are sometimes called temporary restraining orders (TROs).

Drug Names & Medical Terminology

Versed	A fast-acting benzodiazepine medication commonly used to induce sedation, relieve anxiety, or as an anesthetic during medical procedures; generic name midazolam
ampoules	Small, sealed glass containers used to store and preserve single doses of injectable medications or chemicals
fentanyl	A synthetic opioid analgesic that is used to treat severe pain, during or after surgery, and carries a high risk of overdose when used improperly; trade name Sublimaze
Foley bag	A bag used to drain urine from the body when a person is unable to urinate on their own
ketamine	A dissociative anesthetic used medically for anesthesia, pain management, and treatment of severe depression and PTSD; it is also abused recreationally for its hallucinogenic and sedative effects; trade name Ketalar

Narcan	A drug used to reverse the effects of narcotics like fentanyl; generic name flumazenil
Norcuron	A non-depolarizing muscle relaxant used in anesthesia to induce muscle paralysis during surgery or mechanical ventilation; generic name vecuronium
nordiazepam	A metabolite of diazepam (Valium) that has sedative, anxiolytic, and muscle relaxant properties; often used to treat anxiety, insomnia, and muscle spasms
succinylcholine	A fast-acting depolarizing muscle relaxant used in anesthesia to induce temporary paralysis, typically for intubation during surgery; trade name Anectine

CHAPTER 1

WHEN YOU KNOW BEFORE YOU KNOW

When it happens, Tonia, and you see it in your eye, you remember it was me.

—JOHN MEEHAN TO TONIA MEEHAN, 2000

I jumped at the shrill ring of our kitchen phone. Having made it through another long day as a nurse anesthetist, I was home and looking forward to seeing my husband in just a few hours. Both in the medical field—he was studying to be a nurse—it was nice to have a partner who understood my commitment to patients and the toll that work sometimes took on our lives.

In addition to having put in a hard day of work, I was also managing an intense feeling of worry that afternoon. My grandmother hadn't been well, and I was preoccupied thinking about her. But the ringing phone brought me back to reality—in fact, though I didn't realize it at the time, it was an introduction to a new reality I hadn't been expecting.

In 1993, John and I had been married for a few years. I had a full-time job, and he was a full-time student. We had a house that kept us busy with home improvements we'd tackle together. And John loved seeing movies. It seemed like we had to see every movie that came out. Truly, I was glad to join him. What loving wife isn't willing to tag along and enjoy the small things that make her partner happy? We'd have dinner and hang out, talking about our day and our future, just like any newly married couple.

Despite our busy lives, we made time to be together. I assumed that night would be like so many others we had experienced as a married couple, but the phone call changed our plans dramatically.

"Hi, is John there?" a chipper voice asked, after I'd nabbed the phone off the hook and said hello.

"No. He's not available. Can I take a message?"

Disappointment in her voice, the woman asked me if I was John's sister. "No. This is his wife."

Sometimes you know before you know that something is wrong, and this was one of those times. A heavy pause followed, before her stuttering response filled the line.

Growing impatient, I interrupted: "What?"

She eventually managed to tell me her name and that she and John had a mutual friend he was in nursing school with. They had met the night before. John had shared that he lived with his sister and his dying father.

With growing concern, I waited for her to continue. I had a vague recollection that John had made plans to go out with friends the previous night. I thought they may have been studying. I hadn't really been paying that much attention when John had told me, but it wasn't anything out of the ordinary for nursing students. So far, I couldn't see where she was going with this or why she seemed so upset.

Eventually, she blurted out, "I slept with John last night. I didn't know he was married. I think you're married to a con man."

I've lost count of the number of times I've shared this story. I told a close friend that same day, a therapist years later, and eventually reporters, podcasters, and TV show hosts. I can remember answering the phone and our first few exchanges. After that, I can only remember bits and pieces.

She said she and John had gone out. She told me they had sex. For reasons I will never know, he gave her our home phone number before he left. Before the conversation ended, I asked if he had worn a condom.

"No," she replied flatly.

She gave me her name and phone number, and I wrote it down—twice. I planned to give one copy to John, but I hid the other copy in an anesthesia book—page 226, because my birthday is February 26, and I knew I wouldn't forget where I tucked it. Now I realize that this may have been one of the first steps I took to document and uncover John's lies.

I must have continued to respond to her, but the details of that conversation have always been hazy. This was so upsetting and unexpected that I must have gone into shock. I know I kept talking. And I do remember being gracious to her, because—over the decades that John's lies have come to light—I've never felt anger toward any of the women caught up in his deceit. Other than that, I can barely remember the details of what happened.

I have no memory of how our conversation ended, but when I hung up the phone, my first impulse was to call a divorce attorney. It was the '90s, so this meant hauling out the Yellow Pages and flipping through pages and pages of "Do you need a lawyer?" and "Divorce Attorney/Reasonable Fees" advertisements. I dialed one after the other, but it was so late in the day every office was closed.

Defeated, I called a friend and fellow nurse anesthetist who had been through a similar situation for advice. As we talked, I realized the enormity of what I had just learned. I told my friend I didn't think I could go to work the next day. Thankfully, she took care of letting my employer know.

I sat back down at the kitchen table and waited for John to come home.

When he arrived, he glided through the kitchen without a care in the world. With a knot in my stomach, I passed the name and number of the woman who had called just a few hours before across the table.

"Someone called for you," I said, in as calm a voice as I could muster.

I stared at John, looking for any kind of reaction that might indicate guilt—anything that would confirm that what this woman had said was true. But his expression didn't change. He picked the piece of paper up as if it were nothing, said, "Okay, thanks," and started to leave the room.

"Who is she?" I called after him, still trying to steady my voice, not yet ready to tip my hand.

"Just a classmate," he called back.

"That's not what she said," I said flatly.

Now more wary, he returned to the kitchen and asked what I meant.

"She said the two of you slept together last night." There it was. I had finally said it. Now we couldn't go back. Now, I couldn't pretend this wasn't happening.

"Well, that's not true," he said, barely suppressing a laugh.

Again, when I think back on this moment, the details are so faint. When I didn't laugh with him, I remember him looking flustered and denying the affair. John muttered that he needed to take a walk and bolted out the door without giving me even a moment to process that he was leaving.

I was surprised that he would leave in the middle of such an important conversation, but I was so shocked that I didn't say anything. I just let him leave. And then, after about twenty minutes had passed, I realized what had happened.

I grabbed my keys and took off after him.

After driving around in a fog for half an hour, I gave up and returned home.

Where could he have gone? We lived in a small, suburban neighborhood, and he had left on foot. I couldn't understand why I hadn't seen him. But I didn't have much time to wonder, because John came back home, and this time, he had a story to tell.

His demeanor had changed dramatically. He seemed incredibly sad when he took my hand and led me back to the table. He said I needed to sit down. He said there were some things he needed to tell me.

We sat at the kitchen table, and a tearful John started by telling me that what this woman had told me wasn't true. He then told me that, when he was a boy, his brother and a friend had abused him. Confused, I asked John what he was talking about—and what this had to do with the woman who had called earlier.

John ignored my question and talked more about the abuse—something he had never even hinted at before. He implied that the abuse was sexual, but he never specifically told me what had happened. My head was spinning. I knew it was important to let him talk, and so even though I was overwhelmed by the events of the last few hours—and now this startling new information—I patiently listened to what he chose to share. It didn't feel right to ask questions, but he wasn't really making much sense.

I did what I could, and after I consoled John, not thinking he would lie about something like this, I waited for him to connect the dots to the phone call earlier that day. He still hadn't told me what had happened with the woman he had gone out with last night. With some prodding, he went on to say that he had made an unflattering comment about one of the women gaining weight and that it pissed his classmates off. He explained that they were just getting back at him and that they had made it all up.

John knew exactly what to say to me and how to say it. He was so distraught that my empathetic nature kicked into overdrive. Assuming he wouldn't make up such a terrible story about his brother, I was suddenly focused on what to do for John—poor John, a victim of childhood abuse. I had known John for five years at that point and couldn't understand why he had never mentioned this. And I felt so much empathy for him because I imagined that he had held this terrible secret for such a long time.

It was late and it had been an emotional day, so we went to bed early. Drifting off to sleep, I was still trying to process the events of the day. By morning, I had a plan, and I shared it with John.

First, he had to see a counselor. I wanted John to get the help he needed, and I knew it had to be from a professional. I would go with him because this had impacted our marriage, and I saw it as an act of love and solidarity. I was going to be the support John needed at home, and I was going to make sure he got the professional help he needed.

Second, he needed to get rid of his pager. This was before everyone was carrying cell phones, but I still couldn't think of a good reason John would need to carry a pager as a nursing student. After learning more about who John really was, and considering how pagers were used at the time, I think part of the appeal for him was a feeling of importance. Important people who needed to be available at a moment's notice had pagers. That's how John wanted people to see him. Or maybe his pager was how he kept in touch with the multiple women I would eventually learn he was having affairs with. Maybe giving that one woman our home phone number was a simple mistake, and he usually gave out his pager number. I'm not sure what it was about his pager that bothered me at the time, but I knew he didn't need it, and I had hoped not having it would help him stay focused on his schooling and our marriage.

The third thing I told John was that he needed to wear his wedding ring. John had stopped wearing his ring because it would get scuffed up when he lifted weights. While that was obviously disappointing to me, I hadn't ever pressed the issue—but that phone call was the perfect opportunity for me to be honest about how it made me feel.

John agreed to all three new demands, and that made me feel a little better. Once we returned to our busy lives, he only honored one of the requests I made—wearing his ring. My grandmother passed away just a few days after our conversation, and then we were swept up in family and feelings. Our relationship still felt new, and I loved my husband. I had faith it would all work out.

As I sat at that kitchen table with John, I didn't know he was a psychopath.

Almost twenty years later, I would learn about what that really meant—that John was a psychopath. It's not a term used lightly, or to casually describe a person who just makes choices that hurt other people. Psychopaths are chameleon-esque and morally bankrupt. They operate without empathy for others and hurt people without remorse. They seem perfectly normal—even charming—to most people and usually lead perfectly normal lives. To encounter a true psychopath is terrifying.

I had no way of knowing that our marriage would end in a vicious custody battle. I didn't know he was a drug addict working his way into the medical field so that he could more easily divert prescription medications. And I certainly had no way of knowing that, in 2016, I'd receive an alert on my phone telling me he had been killed by a woman he had attacked in broad daylight in Newport Beach, California.

CHAPTER 2

BETTER DAYS

He knew what he was looking for... he was pushing the boundaries right from the start with you. Compliance testing, as I like to call it. Little things, like not taking no for an answer.

—LAURA RICHARDS, THE FIRST WIFE PODCAST

In December of 1988, I was working the second shift at St. Elizabeth's Medical Center in Dayton, Ohio, with my amazing friends and coworkers Sara, Terry, and Chris. Because of the work we did, it was difficult to just clock out and go home. We spent our evenings responding to traumas, operating in high-stress situations, saving lives when we could, and finding ways to cope when we couldn't.

After one of these intense shifts, Terry suggested we check out a new spot we hadn't been to—Shooter's—where we could dance and blow off some steam. I really didn't think that was the energy we were looking for that night, but my friends convinced me. Terry told me it was no big deal—if we didn't like it, we could go somewhere else. A drink and some dancing weren't a bad idea after the night we'd had.

When I walked into that bar, I felt good. I wasn't in a relationship—in fact, I had recently broken up with a long-time boyfriend. And I had just had a rhinoplasty a few months earlier. I had been teased about my nose for my entire life and was enjoying the boost of confidence that came with my new look. I was surrounded by friends and family who loved me, and I had so much happening in my professional life. I had been admitted to a highly competitive anesthesia program and was focused on where my career was heading.

I was engrossed in conversation with my friends, swapping stories and feeling the slow unwinding of our chaotic day. The place wasn't too shady, and the music was good, so we stayed. At one point, I left the group to find the restroom and was stopped by two guys on the way. Jeff, I would later learn, was quite smitten with my coworker Sara, though she wasn't interested in him at all. John, his friend, had set his sights on me.

Decades later I talked to Laura Richards, a criminal behavioral analyst, and asked her opinion on why John pursued me. Of all the women in the bar, what was it about me that stood out?

"You did fit the profile of what John was looking for. He loved what you represented," Laura explained. "You were a nurse. You were in the caring profession. You like looking after people. You're empathetic. You're loyal and responsible. You put others' needs before your own. He knew that from the first conversation with you."

Thinking back to what happened the night I met John, Laura's explanation did make sense. I had to walk past John to get to the bathroom—that part of our encounter was chance, though I'm sure John chose that location intentionally. In retrospect, it seems they were perfectly positioned to stop women all night. He'd want to maximize the chances he'd have to speak to as many women as possible when they would most likely be alone, distracted, and unsuspecting.

When I passed John, he called out to me to grab my attention and we chatted briefly.

The casual atmosphere and jovial tone in his voice made replying easy, but I honestly didn't think much about our first interaction. I hadn't noticed him in the bar earlier. I wasn't thunderstruck when we made eye contact. He just seemed like a friendly guy making conversation.

That quick interaction told John enough of what he needed to know. My willingness to engage with him and my quick smile likely inspired him to try to get my attention again when, as he could easily anticipate, I had to walk past him to return to my group of friends.

Engaging me, he asked where I worked. When I told him, he said he and his friend had been talking to another nurse earlier. This was, of course, my friend Sara. It was a tiny thread, but it was enough to keep our conversation going, so I stopped to chat with him. And in hindsight this was the moment that changed the course of my life forever.

We talked for a while at the bar and danced—still nothing unusual about the evening or our conversation. I do remember a conversation with him at one point that, at the time, seemed meaningless but would later be one of many clues about the deceptive lifestyle he was leading.

Eventually, he needed another drink. Carded by the server, he had removed his license from his wallet, and I playfully grabbed it from him. I immediately noticed that his birth date indicated he was older than twenty-four—the age he had just told me he was. Puzzled, I asked him about the discrepancy.

"Oh, I altered my birth date for my license so that I could get into bars before I was twenty-one. I've really got to get it changed." He wasn't even phased by my question. His confidence, in combination with the fact that I was certainly aware of people using fake IDs, caused me to breeze right past this weird little inconsistency. Plus, why would he lie about his age?

The night wore on, and Jeff, John's ride that evening, was ready to leave. I thought John would take off, too, but he surprised me. He said he wanted to stay. He wanted to keep talking to me.

He asked me to drive him home, and I quickly said no. Having fun with someone you've just met at a bar is one thing—driving them home is another. But John was skilled at pushing boundaries right from the start. He pleaded with me to give him a ride in a playful and flattering way. Rejection was hard for me in normal circumstances, but in this case, I also felt awkward. I think it was because I was young and had limited experience standing firm in my decisions that he was eventually successful in convincing me. I distinctly remember not wanting to give him a ride home, but it felt too uncomfortable to say no.

As we talked, I learned that John and I had more in common than I realized. I told him I was working as a surgical nurse. He shared that he was working in a cath lab as a technician. We were able to talk a bit about working in the medical field. He was so impressed with my career path, and it felt good hearing this stranger share how much he respected the work I was doing. He also told me that he was studying law at the University of Dayton. This was impressive, of course, and not surprising. John was well-spoken and seemed intelligent. We had already talked about our shared interest in learning and how we valued education, so his pursuit of a law degree made perfect sense.

In the parking lot, we said goodnight to my friends. I would later learn that Terry had an uneasy feeling about me leaving with John, but my other friends downplayed his concerns. They convinced him he had nothing to worry about, so he didn't say anything, and I drove John back to the small house he was renting in a student-housing area known as the UD ghetto. John invited me in and, again, after some resistance, I agreed. I really wanted to go home. I had no intention of anything other than dropping John off, but there was something energizing about our meeting.

His obvious interest in me felt good, even if I wasn't entirely sure how I felt about him. He walked me through his cramped house, still chatting animatedly. He was charming, and we were having fun. He picked up a Nerf basketball and challenged me to a game, referencing the small hoop hanging over the door. While we played and laughed, our physical contact increased, both in frequency and intensity. Before long, the basketball game was forgotten, and we were kissing.

I spent the night with John—a man I had just met. I had never done anything like that before, and the next morning I was overwhelmed with feelings of confusion, regret, and embarrassment. John had given me his number, but when I went to work the next day, I thought the best approach would be to just forget it ever happened. It was one night. I regretted it. Maybe I could learn from it. But I certainly wasn't going to let it derail me from my career goals. I was moving to Cincinnati in a month, and my sights were set on advancing my education. I hadn't given John my phone number, so I had no expectation that we would ever cross paths again. It was 1988, so people weren't as easy to find as they are today. But John knew where I worked and, to my surprise, I received an overhead page for a phone call at the hospital the next day.

This moment is another decision point that I still wonder about. I wasn't that interested in John, though his interest in me was definitely feeding my newly found confidence. I was uncomfortable with how our evening had ended and had wanted to forget all about it, but when he tracked me down at work, it made me think maybe we had more of a connection than I realized. He told me I was pretty and that I was a lot of fun. He asked for a chance to take me out on a real date. Was that why I agreed to see him again?

With the passage of time and through conversation with experts, the best answer I can give is that, because of a combination of very specific things, I was compelled to see John again. The first, which is connected to how John and I met in the first place, was my youth and my Midwestern upbringing. People often joke about the kindness and desire to make others happy that is prevalent amongst people from the Midwest, but to a certain extent, it's a very real part of the culture. I was raised not to rock the boat and, at twenty-three years old, I lacked the confidence to turn John down. I couldn't really give him a reason we shouldn't see each other again, so I agreed to a date.

The second reason I agreed to see him again didn't occur to me until much later in my life. Over time, I realized seeing him again helped me justify my decision to stay with him that first night. If John and I really had an incredible, meaningful connection, that made the decision more acceptable. I can't recall feeling an instant connection to John or thinking that I had just met the love of my life. But I do remember feeling a kind of potential for absolution if I had simply been swept off my feet by my one true love.

After our first date, John and I had what I thought was a very normal courtship, as we lived pretty average lives. We were both busy college students who tried to balance homework, date nights, and time with friends. We had time apart and time together, and when we were separated, I had no reason to wonder how John was spending his time.

Years later, I'd talk to his best friend from undergrad, Perry, and learn about how they passed the time in college. Perry recalls the time he spent with John prior to this with great fondness. Perry was a poor and busy pre-med student, while John was a poor and busy pre-law student. When they had free time, they'd sit in beanbag chairs—quintessential college furniture—and dream about their futures.

"We spent a lot of time together. We studied together. We ate probably every dinner together. He was charming, intelligent, and just a very nice guy," Perry remembers.

It helped me to hear these stories about John when I looked back at those early years. I would ultimately learn that he was seeing at least one other woman when I thought we were exclusive, and I think, "What signs did I miss?" People who hear how he lived his life—running frequent and intricate cons—often ask how it's possible I didn't know something was wrong. But John knew how to be the person others needed him to be. He seemed like a great guy to most people, including those he spent a lot of time with, until something happened to make his façade slip. Then he'd have to cut and run. That slip never happened with Perry, and it took nearly ten years to happen with me.

At the end of January 1989, about a month into our relationship, I moved to Cincinnati to begin anesthesia school.

After completing an intense postgraduate program that now requires a doctorate and the successful passing of a board certification exam, I would become a certified registered nurse anesthesiologist (CRNA). CRNAs are advanced practice nurses who administer anesthesia for surgeries, obstetrics, and pain management, and have been doing so for over 150 years. They are the first and longest-standing anesthesia providers in the US. I could not have been more excited to be joining the ranks of this badass profession, but now I also had a new love interest in John that I couldn't ignore.

During my first year of school, I'd travel back to Dayton on the weekends, and we'd spend as much time together as we could. It worked for us, and we were together most weekends throughout that year. In the early days of our relationship, John and I experienced a lot of the same things other couples go through. We talked about our past—our childhood, how we were raised—and our future. I was raised in a stable household, with two parents who modeled what a healthy, loving marriage should look like. My family went to church on Sundays, but more than that, my parents taught me what Catholic values should look like in everyday life.

John shared very different stories from his childhood. He was vague but alluded early on to his family having ties to the mafia. When he initially introduced the idea, I didn't feel uncomfortable or threatened by the idea at all. I wasn't impressed, either, which I think may have been John's goal at the time. It also seems likely that telling me he was tied to a dangerous crime family would be one more way to keep me from wanting to meet his parents or siblings.

My childhood was filled with examples of imperfect but long-lasting relationships. My parents were both hard workers and functioned as a good team. They had traditional roles, with my mom primarily taking care of the cooking and cleaning and my dad handling the yard, the cars, and all of the repairs that come with having a nice house. We always had dinner together around the kitchen table at five o'clock sharp, where everyone shared their day—the good and the bad. The dinner table is where I learned to be a good human, and our home is where I learned that I wanted to be a wife and a mother.

John expressed a strong desire for the same kind of life, but it seemed our similar dreams emerged from very different experiences. John shared that his parents had divorced and that they were both incredibly selfish people. He shared that his mother was addicted to pills and that his father was an alcoholic. His siblings had all chosen similarly questionable paths in their lives. Month after month, when we'd have conversations over dinner or on the phone, and he'd share small bits of information about his family, it made sense that he felt as strongly as I did about the importance of leading a life rooted in Christian values, where your family is your first priority, and you work every day to put kindness out into the world. I loved that we were both Catholic.

Our courtship was uneventful. When I did question John about something he told me that seemed a bit off or didn't make sense, he always had a quick explanation that made perfect sense. Even with the benefit of hindsight, when I look back on our time together, I can't honestly identify many instances where it would have been reasonable at the time for me to think John was lying to me.

I know now that most of what John shared about his family was either exaggerated or just plain untrue. Yes, his parents had divorced, and his father was reportedly a big drinker and often running various scams to bring in extra money. His brother had adopted some of those same illegal practices, but his sisters had separated themselves from the Meehan criminal activity and had families of their own. My daughters could have met their aunts and cousins, so why did John work so hard to keep us apart? And perhaps even more of a mystery, why didn't his sisters ever try to reach out to me? Time would tell.

Only when our marriage began to dissolve after nearly ten years did I begin to question John's stories. I realized I had very little to corroborate anything he had told me. When my boyfriend, who became my fiancé and then my husband, shared painful memories from his childhood, I didn't ask him for proof. I simply believed him. It wasn't until after our separation, when I uncovered one lie and then another, that I began to question if anything he had ever told me was the truth.

It was almost unbearable to realize that, as early as our first dates, John was telling stories that would ensure I would only hear his version of how he grew up. Each lie he told was another barrier to me ever having a conversation with someone who could potentially reveal a truth about his past. He painted a picture of his father as threatening and abusive—someone I would never want to contact. He described his mother as an addict who'd try to force herself into our lives. He said she was toxic and warned me never to open the door for her. His siblings, he assured me, were all self-destructive, awful people. He told me his brother was an addict and one of his sisters had already been married four times—he didn't want any of them in our children's lives.

When I was first learning about John, just like anyone dating someone new, I was beginning to believe that he was a man who had defied the odds. He had come from terrible circumstances and, instead of feeling sorry for himself or taking the easy way out and joining his family's criminal activity, he broke free. I had compassion and respect for how he was fighting to make something of himself.

But when we separated a decade later, I'd lay in bed at night, or have a quiet moment at work, and ponder the same question people would ask me in the wake of our divorce and again after John's highly publicized death: How was he able to get away with so many lies for such a long time?

While we were dating and during the early years of our marriage, it was easy for him. I was a loving wife who believed I was in a healthy marriage. When my life partner told me something about his family or his past, I believed him because I didn't have any reason not to. When he said he was protecting our family from his, I saw the fierce commitment he had to us. Still, I wondered why his mother and sisters kept their distance. Why didn't someone warn me? In the early part of my investigation into John's past, that had bothered me. It just didn't make sense that, for so long, he could keep us separated. Eventually I would realize that the fear I felt about John when we separated was the same fear they had felt about him their entire lives.

John and me at a friend's wedding in 1989.

CHAPTER 3

FAMILY TIES

He's a phantom. An apparition. Second cousin to Harvey the Rabbit. I conjured him out of thin air. He doesn't exist, except on paper.

—TIM ROBBINS AS ANDY DUFRESNE, THE SHAWSHANK REDEMPTION

Getting to know people—boyfriends and girlfriends, neighbors, coworkers—usually involves exchanging stories over time. There's the standard "first meeting" topics—where you're from and how you spend your time—but after that, what we learn about each other is often influenced by what comes up naturally in conversation. A scene from a movie reminds you of a moment from your childhood, so you share that story with your partner. You run into an old friend, so you begin to reminisce. You may even steer a conversation you're having toward something that makes you look good to someone you want to impress.

I thought I was experiencing all of these normal things with John in our first year of dating. To my eventual surprise, I'd learn that, while I was sharing true stories about myself, he was carefully crafting a false image of who he really was.

Thinking about my earliest interactions with John today means trying to remember conversations from decades ago, without email or text messages to refresh my memory. Thankfully, I have a few letters, some notes, and my own journal. A funny thing about memory is that, with reminders and some work, small pieces will come back, and sometimes those small pieces help bigger pieces fall into place.

A few specific conversations are burned in my memory. In most cases, they seemed relatively insignificant at the time they happened. Later, when I began to suspect that John had been lying to me, those specific conversations started to come back to me. I'd try to separate the truth from the lies. I would wonder what his goal had been. What could he have possibly hoped to gain by working so hard to deceive me? And sometimes I wonder if I ever exaggerated anything myself to impress him. It's something we all do naturally, isn't it? We paint ourselves in the most favorable light we can when we're getting to know someone. Then, once we realize we may have found the one person we want to spend the rest of our lives with, we share our whole selves. I believe people should be able to share the best and worst parts of themselves with that one other person with the hope that we will still be loved and desired despite our faults. But John was a psychopath. He lived his entire life lying and manipulating others, and that means he never connected with another person on the most intimate level.

The other challenge that comes with looking back on my early years with John is that my feelings toward him have changed so drastically. I initially found the stories he told me interesting, sad, impressive, or heartwarming because I was falling in love with him, and I had no reason to question what he was saying. Now I know that much of what he shared were lies. And they weren't the little white lies we all tell to impress someone on a date, or the kinds of things we might misremember because time has passed.

Today I know that, from the start of our relationship, John's goal was to carefully construct a version of himself that I would fall in love with, without question, and follow blindly until he didn't need or want me anymore. As I have learned more about how psychopaths work, I have learned an important term: data mining.

When a psychopath is data mining, their conversation partner feels like they're having a normal conversation. They may even feel like they're talking to someone who's really interested in their thoughts and ideas—someone who really wants to get to know them.

"What's most important to you in a partner?"

"What are your goals?"

Data mining questions don't jump out at you. There are rarely any red flags associated with the topics. They are innocuous, open-ended questions meant to uncover more about you, so that the person interested in manipulating you can zero in on what's important to you, what upsets you, and what you care about. They may not always learn everything they need to know, but you will tell them plenty without worrying about anything you've shared.

How could data mining have helped John? Think about the very normal question someone might ask on a date about what's important to you in a partner. When any woman answered that question for John, she provided him with a blueprint for how he needed to act to deceive them. If being courteous and respectful was important to them, he was sure to open doors and genuinely thank the valet. If work ethic was most important, he was sure to talk about how he worked through college and paid his own way. Whatever she shared, he could mirror.

And what about women telling John about their goals? How could that be used against them? When we share our goals, we often end up sharing our vulnerabilities too. Whether we realize it or not, telling someone about a goal we want to achieve often reveals why that goal is important to us and what in our personal history has shaped that belief. If your goal is to run a marathon, there's probably a reason physical fitness is important to you—a fear of a specific illness, a parent who struggled with poor health habits all their life, or a former partner who ridiculed you for your weight. If your goal is to obtain a specific position in an organization, there's a good chance you feel like you've been overlooked or even that you feel insecure about your professional accomplishments. These common questions are nothing to be concerned about in everyday conversations, but from a psychopath's perspective, they have the potential to reveal information that will later be used to manipulate you.

Now, I understand that when John talked to people, including me, and asked general questions, he was able to agree with whatever the response was, strengthening his connection with that girlfriend, coworker, or even acquaintance. Most people who knew John described him as very charming, and if he was frequently data mining, that would be the reason why. Data mining can look like you're an engaged, unselfish listener.

But he would also remember what people shared with him and build on what he perceived a person's beliefs to be.

If someone shared that they were nervous about an increase in the crime rate, he could use that fear to make them reliant on him for a ride home. If they're jealous of their sibling's success, he can mention that sibling's accomplishments to distract them when he needs them to be off their game. The ways a psychopath can use data mining to harm others are endless and, unless you know what you are looking for, nearly impossible to detect.

Thinking back on our time together, there were moments when I can see now what John was doing and even when he was lying. Of course, at the time, that wasn't the case. For one thing, when John and I were dating and even while we were married, verifying a story with an internet search wasn't as easy as it is today. But perhaps an even bigger factor is that I've always been a pretty honest person, and I saw everything he did through an honest person's lens. It didn't cross my mind that the things he was doing could be tied to bad intentions.

Curiously, when I think about all the things I learned about John in the first years that I knew him and compare them to what I eventually learned was true, only some of his lies make sense. Some of his stories I would call "functional"—how he got from where he was to where he wanted to be. But others still make no sense at all, and I question if sometimes he just lied for the sport of getting away with fooling people.

The most troubling lies are the ones that truly demonstrate his warped perception of the world. One example of this slow deception was when my relationship with John became more serious, and we shared information about our upbringings. Like most couples, we talked about family dynamics, religion, and what we wanted for our own families. One lie John told me that I've always found especially strange was that his mother, Dolores, was Jewish, though he and his siblings were raised as

Catholics, like his father. When we separated, I learned that John's father was Catholic and John had been raised in the Catholic church, but his mother had also been a practicing Catholic her entire life. When I first discovered this, I briefly questioned my own memory: Did I imagine John telling me that his mother was Jewish? No, I was sure of what he had told me. And John's mother being Jewish didn't matter to me at all, so why would he tell such a meaningless lie?

When I consider the timing of when John shared this, what he had learned about me, and what he was trying to accomplish, it makes a little more sense. John knew that I was raised in a Catholic home and that my faith was important to me. At that point, he even knew that I wanted to raise my children in the Catholic church. He had to identify ways to stay close to me and to isolate me from his family, and I believe he thought our difference in religion would make me feel like I had even less in common with his mother.

But I think there was another reason. The more stories I hear about how John spoke to other people about his mother, the more I think he felt that her not being Catholic like the rest of his family was just one more way to separate from her, to hurt her, even if she didn't know he had said that. Even if he knew it was a lie and even if he didn't think anyone really cared, I think there's a good chance that he told me that particular lie out of spite.

I never had the chance to ask him—and I doubt he would have told me the truth—but it seems clear now that he thought telling me his mother was Jewish would make me less likely to try to connect with her. He knew it would take time to build a case against his family and that one day I may be tempted to reach out to his mother. This was one of the first lies that he told me about his family in an attempt to turn me against them, with John's ultimate goal being that I would never want to contact them, keeping so many of his other lies safe.

Another important thing I've learned is that serial liars often root their stories in as much truth as possible. I would learn over time that John did this often, and that the base of truth likely helped him hide his lies. For example, when he talked about his brother Dan, whom I never had the chance to meet, he talked about Dan's terrible drug problem. He told me his brother was someone we shouldn't be around. He was emphatic that we shouldn't meet and left me with the feeling that he was acting as my protector, keeping me from his brother. John, knowing how I felt about illegal drug use, likely saw this bit of information about Dan as a way to ensure I'd never reach out to Dan on my own.

The truth was that Dan had been an addict—his drug use was what killed him. Of course, it was years before I learned the role John's family believed he played in Dan's addiction. Eventually, John's sisters helped me understand who Dan really was. He also seemed to be a product of his father's manipulation. The difference was that no one saw their brother Dan in the manipulative and evil way they saw John. Their brother Dan was far from perfect, but he was loved.

It's also important to remember that when you are involved with a con artist, you can have hundreds of interactions with them that are perfectly normal. They pick up milk on the way home from the store because you asked them to. They suggest seeing a movie you really want to see. They have friends at work who tell them funny stories that they then relay to you.

But it's the dramatic stories that make headlines, so it's easy for people to forget that the true, simple conversations happen between the lies, making those lies harder to spot. My story is a perfect example of this. When people watch the *Dirty John* series or even when they listen to my podcast, they see and hear more about the lies he told than the everyday conversations we had that were just part of our normal lives. John didn't always complain about his family and his early years. He spoke fondly of an uncle and shared happy memories of his maternal grandfather, who passed away early in our relationship. I remember John traveling to Northern California for the funeral and taking some things from his grandfather's house to remember him by. These are the types of stories that few people know about John, and they're the stories that even I have to dig deep to recount in detail. When trying to explain how manipulative people get away with as much as they do, the stories in between the lies are as important to share as the lies themselves. Discovering all of his deception was so painful, it became almost impossible to remember anything normal or human about our relationship.

I never really had the chance to connect with John's sisters when we were married, and some people thought that was strange. They had grown up with John, so when he told them not to reach out to me, they understood just how important it was for them to follow his very clear demand. But once John and I separated, they were both eager to talk to me.

Even though there was always an underlying concern that John would retaliate against them, they were quick to share their stories. When we were married, John would have seen a relationship with them as a risk to his lies being uncovered. But at the time, their distance only reinforced the ideas that John had planted in my head years ago.

John described his sister Donna as unreliable and a careless spender, marrying and divorcing so often that he could barely keep up. Once I met Donna, I quickly realized that wasn't the case. She was a kind and generous person, interested in hearing about my girls. The thoughtless, shallow woman John had warned me about was nowhere in sight.

Throughout our marriage, I heard stories about how selfish his sister Karen was—the real "brat" in the family. That, too, I learned was untrue. In fact, Karen and her siblings shared stories that made me realize it was John who often would act out. A particularly cruel story I heard a few times from John's family occurred when Karen, younger than John, was attending the same school as her older brother. Did he look out for her? Just the opposite—he sought her out and tormented her, knocking her books out of her hands as she walked down the hallway. It was no wonder he was so committed to keeping us apart. No one wants their spouse to hear stories like that, even if they were just a kid in high school. Eventually, I would hear stories of how John bullied his classmates when he was in nursing school, realizing bullying was likely a pattern he followed throughout his life.

Michael, John's younger half-brother, was the sibling he seemed most fond of, despite being much younger than John and a product of his mother's second marriage—a marriage John had very hard feelings about. Being younger, Michael knew fewer secrets than the others, I'm sure. I only met him once, but I thought the relationship they had was wonderful. They picked on each other in a fun and loving way. Michael was the sweetest, and John seemed to genuinely enjoy spending time with him. But even conversations with Michael were rare. It made sense that he would want to start a new life away from these people. It was impressive that he had come from such a terrible environment and was now such an amazing person.

Separate from his family, there were other lies that John crafted. Again, when I consider why he told them, some of them do make sense to me. Today I can see what he was likely trying to do, even though it didn't seem strange to me at the time. One time, he shared, out of the blue, that he had an $80,000 trust fund. I had never asked about his financial situation, and we weren't yet at the stage where we were talking about combining our finances, so I hadn't prompted the lie. Why would he offer that information? Maybe because, to John, money was power. He believed having money made him more impressive. So, even though I hadn't been wondering about his financial security, he offered up that piece of information anyway, presumably hoping that I would see him in a more favorable light.

When he lied to me about having a trust fund, I suppose I did feel a kind of happiness for him. It's always nice to hear that someone you care about has financial security and support, and it showed me that someone really loved him. But I don't think it had the exact effect he was hoping for. I was on my way to a successful career as a nurse anesthetist. I wasn't seeking financial security from a partner. I don't think I responded as he had hoped, but he stuck to his lie. I suppose there was no taking it back.

What I'll always wonder is if he ever thought about what would happen when he had to produce the money he said he had. A trait common amongst psychopaths is living in the moment and rarely thinking about the future, so I suspect he either never considered what would happen if I asked him to produce the money, or he just planned to deal with that situation if and when it came up. Years later, I heard stories about women he'd talked to about his substantial wealth and how he hid the truth from them. The stories more people know about are how he convinced Debra, his second wife, that I was responsible for tying up his finances, that he had to hide money from me, that I was bankrupting him. Just as he told me his family was terrible, he told her that I was terrible. It seemed John moved from person to person, often making whoever had last been the important people in his life—first his family members, then me and our kids—the next explanation for whatever problems he was having.

I have realized, too, that even John himself probably didn't always know what was the truth and what was a lie. Early in our marriage, when the woman with whom he had cheated on me called our house, he told me that he had been abused when he was younger. Did he make that up? Was it, at least in part, true?

In other cases, though, I know he actively chose to exaggerate stories to serve his own purpose. One of the biggest mysteries I'll probably never unravel is about Bill, John's father. After talking to John's sisters, I do believe they all had a difficult childhood and that Bill was a toxic influence in their family throughout their childhood and in their adult lives. One memory John shared that his sisters remembered as well was the day their mother left. As teenagers, shocked at the sudden loss of their mother, they sat across from Bill as he told them that she had left because of them. As a mother who has had to have a lot of difficult conversations with her children about the actions of their father, I know how stressful those conversations are and how tempting it is to let your own fears and frustrations overwhelm you. But I can't see myself ever saying something so hurtful to my girls. I can only imagine how hearing that from his father must have affected John and his siblings.

I never got the sense that John processed his parents' actions the same way that I did. He described his family as normal up until his parents separated. Despite sharing stories about how his father stabbed him with a serving fork at a picnic and put his life at risk by using him to run cons, John seemed to blame his mother for all that went wrong in their family. While he seemed equally angry with his father, he was also devoted to him. Perhaps Dolores was sheltering the children and they didn't understand what was happening in their family or how their father had played a role.

After both John and Dan had died, their sisters shared more about when their mother left for the last time. Dolores had left Bill before, but she always returned when Bill begged her to come back. Time and time again, she overlooked not only minor acts of disrespect but also extreme abuse. Karen and Donna recounted stories that ranged from Bill saying he was going to get candy during a movie and simply abandoning Dolores in the theater to Bill storming out of the house after a fight, turning the gas stove on before he left, presumably with the hope that Dolores, pregnant with Dan, would succumb to the fumes. Dolores overlooked these minor and major attacks until one day she'd had enough.

Dolores had left Bill for good and was in a new relationship. As his daughters tell the story, Bill sent someone to rough up the boyfriend and scare Dolores into coming home. The opposite occurred—she was so scared, she and her boyfriend moved to Hawaii. Knowing what I do about Bill, I am sure his plan backfiring infuriated him. And understanding John like I do today, I can see that Bill passed that fury at Dolores on to John.

As I found out more about the experiences John had throughout his life and all the things he had lied about, I didn't find any justification for what he did to us and our family. But that wasn't what I was looking for. I was trying to understand why a person would make the choices he did. I was hoping to better understand John so that I could better understand myself and our shared history. Over time, I've also learned more than I ever thought I would about the legal system and how it can be manipulated.

When I was first dating John, he seemed like a great guy. He was smart and made me feel like he cared about me. He understood my values and told me we had shared beliefs. But how did he really view the world, even back when we first met?

In an interview with the *LA Times*, John's sister Karen summed up what her brother learned from an early age. "If anybody did anything to John, my dad would tell us, 'You go there with a stick and take care of it.' It's the Brooklyn mentality of 'you fight, you get even.' If you want to get back at somebody, you don't get back at them, you get back at their family." It would take years for me to learn about his revenge tactics, but eventually I would uncover more of John's devious behavior than I could have imagined.

CHAPTER 4

A FRIEND LIKE JOHN

I hated the guy's guts.

—JOE, A FRIEND BETRAYED BY JOHN

Most of the stories the public knows about John involve the women he spent time with, but when I started looking into his past, I realized that fear, manipulation, and betrayal were themes in every relationship in his life—to varying degrees, of course, depending on what John needed from the person and how quickly something happened to reveal his true nature.

One person who knew John—as much as anyone could really know John—was his friend Joe. The two met at a young age and spent a lot of time together just hanging out. Hearing Joe describe their early years together, they sound just like the kind of guys we all went to high school and college with. They went out on double dates and to parties together. But eventually the two got into some serious trouble.

Joe thought John was a rule follower at first. Initially, he seemed to be a good student who wouldn't have anything to do with illegal drugs. John started working at a hospital and, to Joe, appeared to be a normal college student with a job and a full course load. But slowly that began to change. When they were roommates, Joe noticed that John was oddly secretive, locking his bedroom door when everyone else in the house left theirs wide open. Eventually Joe figured out that John's secrecy was related to his other part-time job: drug diversion.

We can't know when John discovered how easy it was for him to steal drugs from the hospital where he was working, but it seems clear that he discovered the opportunity during his college years and honed his skills as a dealer over time. Joe recalls John bringing home Valium to sell—at that time, he still didn't seem to be using drugs himself. I'm sure that not getting caught emboldened John, and we know that he expanded the kinds of drugs he would steal and sell.

In the 1980s, liquid cocaine was used by physicians to control nosebleeds and as an analgesic. It's likely that John, working as an orderly in a hospital, would have had access to liquid cocaine that wasn't properly disposed of, like what was left in a vial after the anesthetic had been given to a patient, but he may have also found ways to steal full vials without hospital staff being able to trace the theft back to him. Today these drugs are strictly controlled, but in the early '80s, when we were still learning about how people were feeding their addictions, John saw and capitalized on the opportunity to begin diverting legal drugs as a way to make extra money.

Joe, like so many of us, found himself in questionable situations with John and admits that he and John didn't always make the best choices. One series of small bad choices eventually snowballed into serious consequences for Joe. As usual, at the expense of others, John manipulated a situation to escape unscathed, leaving Joe in so much trouble with law enforcement that he would end up in prison. It reminds the rest of us that no one needs a friend like John.

Joe remembered John worrying about money, which not everyone knew about. Outwardly, John didn't appear to have any money problems, and the cars he drove often made him look like he was living more comfortably than he actually was. But to his close friends, he often complained about how his family didn't help him financially and that he was constantly in need of cash.

He wanted to attend medical school, but cost was an obstacle. How would he cover tuition? The two young men started looking for gigs on the side, and John started selling cocaine. As Joe describes it, John was a successful dealer. That's not surprising, considering how charismatic he was. John bragged to Joe that he was cutting the cocaine he had to half the grade it was when he got it, continuously increasing his profit margins. He'd have calls and visitors in the middle of the night. In a short period of time, John had built a reputation as a dealer and was experiencing success in the illegal drug trade.

Joe saw how well John was doing, and when John approached him one day to get him in on a deal, he jumped at the chance. Joe just needed to get three kilos of cocaine to John—John already had buyers. Even though John was much more connected, Joe didn't think for a minute that there was anything suspicious about the request. Excited for the opportunity, he said he had some connections and would set it up.

On March 3, 1983, Joe's contacts came through, and cocaine was brought to La Hacienda, an upscale restaurant in

Los Gatos that has since closed. Seemingly out of nowhere, ATF burst through the doors. A patron of the restaurant described the scene to a local reporter from the *Los Gatos Weekly* as "just like Clint Eastwood. They told us not to move. I was sitting there with a client. It scared the hell out of us."

They made five arrests in the restaurant, including Joe and John, and led them out with pillowcases over everyone's heads, eventually bringing them all to different departments for questioning so no one would know who the informant was. But in that moment, Joe knew it had to be John.

Later, Joe asked John, "Why'd you do it? Why would you do that to me?" John's only reply was that he "had to do it." He told Joe he had been busted with half an ounce of cocaine, and, if charged, it would be a felony. He wouldn't be able to get into medical school with a felony on his record, so he saw no option other than betraying his friend. Ultimately, John would receive a minor charge with no jail time, while Joe would go to prison.

The drug bust at La Hacienda happened in 1983, five years before I met John. The bust was the largest in the county's history, but I was living in Ohio and certainly hadn't heard about it. Even if I had heard the story and remembered it five years later, I would have had no reason to believe John was connected to it. In today's hyperconnected world, it's hard for people to understand that I could have known John for as long as I did without this ever coming up. So I'll explain exactly what John did—and a few circumstances that just happened to work in his favor—to separate himself from his first major drug arrest.

First, John betrayed Joe—this was what John did and would continue to do to the people he knew for the rest of his life. When I learned more about John, I learned more about police investigations, and it's true what you see on TV. The police do make deals with certain people so that they can apprehend more dangerous criminals. When John got caught and was offered a deal, he took it. That was the best opportunity he had to avoid serious charges, and I'm sure he didn't think twice before sacrificing Joe and others to secure a better result for himself.

Another consistent practice John used was to continually erase periods of time from his personal history, which caused enough confusion to distract from or even entirely mask the reality of what he had done. When John was arrested for possession of cocaine in 1983, he was twenty-four years old. When I met him five years later, he told me he was twenty-four years old. I'm not sure if I would have ever heard about the drug bust in Los Gatos thousands of miles away, but even if I had, I had no way to tie him to what had happened. Eventually, writing and rewriting his personal history would catch up with him, but for a long time, John simply changed his story if it didn't serve his purpose, changing his name and birth date, making it nearly impossible to keep track of his crimes.

And finally, John had his criminal record expunged. Even before we met, John had planned on working in a field that would require a criminal background check. He was always planning on law school or medical school. He knew he would need to get his drug conviction removed if he was going to be successful.

It's a little scary to think about people like John getting caught and then being able to erase all records of their conviction, so it's good to remind ourselves that it isn't a common occurrence. The requirements for having your record expunged vary by state and are dependent on the seriousness of the charge. I'll never know exactly what happened, but John requested that his record be cleared, and it was. It's likely that he convinced a judge that it was a minor offense, he was cooperative with law enforcement, and he was on his way to doing great things in the world that would be hindered by this minor infraction from his youth. I can see how convincing his argument could have been, and I understand why a judge would have looked at John and seen a young man with tremendous potential. They couldn't have known what removing that drug charge would mean or the damage John would eventually cause, in part because he was able to work in medicine.

Hearing Joe's story also made me think about how, years later, John would steal drugs from the hospital and hide them in the house we shared. Since John and I were both CRNAs at the time, we had access to the same drugs. While I'm sure ease of access and his addiction were his primary motivators for stealing various medications from hospitals, I can also see now that he likely had another plan too. He knew no one could prove the drugs were his because of what he stole and where he kept them. To John, Joe and I were a great way to create confusion if he was caught. Fortunately for me, John was never able to pin any of his crimes on me. Because Joe had broken the law, he wasn't so lucky.

Because his record had been cleared, if I had been suspicious of John at any point in our relationship and had a background check done, this very serious offense wouldn't have even shown up. But John doesn't get full credit for avoiding serious charges. Several other forces helped John hide his bad behavior.

The media in 1983 was very different from the way it is today. Even when I was looking for this story decades later with the internet at my fingertips, I couldn't find it. Eventually, with the help of a research librarian who looked through archived local newspapers—none of which were available online—I found two small references to the event. The twenty-four-hour news cycle was just getting started, and social media wasn't a thing. If it had been, I might have heard about what happened, but even then, I probably wouldn't have known about John's connection to the raid.

Here's part of the *Los Gatos Weekly* report.

> *"Police seize cocaine, arrest 5 in local bust"*
>
> *Five pounds of cocaine, with a street value of $1 million, was seized by Los Gatos police last week, in what authorities are calling the biggest drug bust of the town's history. Los Gatos detectives, in conjunction with the county's Allied Narcotics Enforcement Team, arrested five men for sale of cocaine Thursday at 6:45 p.m. in the bar of La Hacienda Inn, 18440 Saratoga-Los Gatos Road. The five suspects, whose names are being temporarily withheld at the request of police, were booked into county jail on charges of possession and sale of cocaine. Bail for each suspect has been set at $250,000.*

John had clearly been in serious trouble, but hardly any media outlets had picked up the story. And the police never released the names of the people involved to the public. With today's media, it seems like anonymity is impossible, so it's hard to imagine no one ever learned that John was one of the five people arrested. But I was looking for a connection to John and could barely confirm that the story happened, much less that he was there.

I did a little more digging and learned that it's very possible for raids to be conducted without the media hearing about it. To the average person, raids and arrests seem like such major events. But the only way the media hears about them is if someone involved alerts them. Essentially, if a person who has knowledge of the event shares what happened with the media, a reporter may pursue the story. Or if someone from the media happens to be in a courthouse, they could hear about a bust and choose to cover it. But the ATF and FBI don't regularly issue press releases for every arrest.

This makes sense now, of course. You hear all the time about how warrants are sealed and identities are protected. It's frustrating to experience when you're trying to learn about a dangerous person, but these cases are often complex, and decisions have to be made to serve the community and often to protect innocent people. Sometimes the guilty end up benefiting, too.

When I learned about John's drug bust, I was shocked. I'm sure anyone would be surprised to learn that someone they knew well had been involved in such a serious crime, but it was especially upsetting to me that John had been an integral player in distributing illegal drugs within his community. As medical professionals, he and I both knew about the destruction that drug use can bring to individuals, their families, and even entire communities. John acting as a drug dealer, even years before we met, was almost unimaginable. Even though I understood the facts, it took time for me to process all that I was learning.

When I first spoke with Joe directly, he couldn't have been more kind. I reached out to see if he would share his experience with John with me and the world on the podcast I was putting together. I didn't know if he, like me, would want to tell his story to show people what it means to interact with a psychopath. I wouldn't have blamed him if he just wanted to forget the whole thing. But if I was going to help listeners understand how John manipulated the people closest to him, I had to at least try.

Today, when Joe talks about John, you can hear the hurt in his voice. He clearly regrets the mistakes he made when he was younger. But Joe, like me and my daughters, is living a happy life today. He is surrounded by people who love him and support him. John betrayed him, but he didn't stop him from living a rich and happy life.

CHAPTER 5

THE REALITY OF LOVE

Love does not delight in evil but rejoices with the truth.

—1 CORINTHIANS 13:6

In 1989, while John was in California working as a law clerk for the summer, he went with his sister Donna to choose a center stone for my engagement ring. I didn't even know that he was in contact with Donna, since he always told me that he had little to no communication with his family. Eventually I learned that he did stay in contact with them, and he only separated us to keep them from undoing all of the lies he had told me about himself.

The engagement ring John gave me will always make me wonder. Years later, while John and I were still married, I took my ring to a jeweler because a small stone had fallen out and needed to be replaced. The jeweler looked at the ring and then he looked at me and asked, somewhat delicately, "You know this is fake, right?"

Reflexively, I said that yes, I did know the stone wasn't real. But I'm positive he saw the blood drain from my face. I was humiliated. He had the decency to pretend like he believed me. I left with my wedding ring, wondering why John would have bought me a fake diamond. I, of course, gave John the benefit of the doubt and assumed he really wanted me to have a nice ring but couldn't afford it. Now, hearing Donna's story, I understood that, at one point, the original stone for my ring had been real. What had happened?

A few years after I learned that the diamond in my ring wasn't real, John said he wanted to put a nicer center stone in my ring, and he did. He never admitted that the stone I had was fake, but it didn't matter to me and I wanted to save him the embarrassment. At the time, I thought he was still sparing my feelings and didn't want me to know that my original diamond had been a fake. When we divorced, I think John may have regretted his decision to swap out that stone. He was adamant that he should get my ring back, but my attorney quickly squashed that request.

With a real or fake diamond—I'll never know—John asked me to marry him after a year of dating. The proposal was simple, in my apartment in Cincinnati. It was just the two of us, and it was as lovely as I could have hoped for. I loved the simplicity of it, and I felt like I was at the start of an amazing life. I was making great professional strides, and I was marrying a wonderful man. Everything was falling into place.

Most brides-to-be will tell you that the memories of planning their wedding are largely a blur, with vivid memories here and there. I would agree—I can see snapshots of conversations, dress fittings, and meetings with wedding vendors. But mostly

I remember the overarching positive feelings I had through the whole beautifully chaotic process.

My parents gave us a modest budget for the wedding, but I knew John and I were going to have to spend carefully and still contribute something financially. I was up for the challenge and loved every minute of the planning process. I did have help from my younger sister and my bridesmaids, and at the time, I even felt like John was as involved as he could be.

I was in anesthesia school in Cincinnati while planning the wedding, and we were getting married in Dayton. That meant I was focused on being a student during the week—up early, in class or clinicals during the day, homework at night. Then, on the weekend, I'd make the hour drive to Dayton to look at wedding venues, pick flowers, and complete all of the tasks that come with planning a traditional wedding.

John had been in law school in Ohio, but because of delays related to his financial aid, he couldn't attend the next semester and was scrambling to figure out what to do. With his father's help, he secured a job in California and started going to law school. So he was working as a law clerk during the day and in school for his law degree at night, but we were a few thousand miles apart. We would talk on the phone often and I'd give him updates, like when the church was reserved or the flowers were chosen. He'd listen to me as I recounted conversations with the caterer or how one of my bridesmaids had an opinion different from the others. He wasn't there with me or even really helping to plan the wedding, but it felt like he was present and as involved as he could be.

Over the two years that we dated, hearing him share his experiences growing up and even how he described his siblings as adults had prepared me for the worst. I would be there for John, and we wouldn't let his family ruin our day.

To my surprise, John didn't want to talk about what we could do to make sure his family didn't ruin the wedding. And he didn't want to leave them off the guest list either. John told me that he did want to invite his immediate family. He wanted them to know about me and the wedding and that we were starting our lives together. But he wanted to send the invitations so close to the wedding date that they wouldn't be able to attend. I knew they were all far enough away that the plan would probably work. Flight, hotel, and any other travel arrangements would be difficult and expensive at the last minute. So that's what he did, and his plan worked. No one from John's family made it to our wedding.

Weddings bring up a lot of emotions, and not all of them are good. While I didn't agree with John's approach of excluding his family, I did understand it. I thought he was doing his best to manage his own feelings and to make sure no one ruined our day. Now I can see that he suggested that approach because it involved his ideal kind of deception—one that would allow John to claim that he was blameless and that others had wronged him.

His immediate family wasn't the only noticeable absence, though. Days before the wedding, John told me that his best man, Perry, wouldn't be at the wedding. His grandfather had passed away, and he would be with his family. It was nothing for me to worry about, because he was just going to ask one of his other groomsmen to take on the role. It didn't seem to upset John, and I was glad that he already had groomsmen who could step up.

Years later I would learn that Perry, who knew John was living in California, had every intention of being there, but didn't receive the invitation with the wedding details until it was too late for him to make the trip.

"I never knew the wedding was in Ohio," Perry, who had been living in Arizona at the time of our wedding, recalled. "I think it was less than a week before the wedding that he told me it was in Ohio. My plan had been to just drive to California for the weekend." Perry was in med school at the time and had finals, making the long trip to Ohio impossible on such short notice.

I'll never know exactly what happened, but I suspect that John was just careful not to specify where the wedding would be until it was so close to the date that Perry wouldn't be able to join us. All of the other groomsmen got the information they needed, so John knew to share the details. It was the same technique he used with his family, but this time, he didn't let me in on it. Perry and I were both in the dark.

But what could John have been worried about? Some of his groomsmen had been on double dates with John while I thought we were in a monogamous relationship. Some even admitted that they were surprised to hear that John was engaged because John "was one to kiss and tell, and he liked the ladies." Of course, they never said anything to me. They probably later reflected on whether or not they should have. But at the time, John believed his groomsmen wouldn't rat him out. Since Perry didn't know about his cheating, was he too much of a risk?

Despite the challenges we had with the guest list and bridal party, the day was perfect. I started the morning with a hair appointment that involved weaving a rather elaborate veil headpiece into my hair. Looking at the photos now, my hair was a lot. But at the time, I was perfectly in fashion, and I felt amazing.

I met my bridesmaids at my parents' house, and we all piled into a limo that dropped us off at the church so we could finish getting ready. My sister, Beth, who was my maid of honor, and my bridesmaids, Kathy, Sara, and Julia, had a wonderful morning getting ready for the wedding. The accommodations at the church were pretty standard. A multipurpose room had been converted into a space for me to get ready in, with a makeup table and a full-length mirror. We were so joyful, laughing with nervous excitement. And then the moment arrived.

My dad walked me down the aisle at 2:30 sharp. I remember John standing at the altar and tugging on the bottom of his vest. *He's making it just right*, I thought, filled with happiness at the realization that John was as committed to our marriage as I was.

Faith has always been important to me, and that day, I believed it was equally important to John. Our shared belief was one of the things that made our relationship so strong and what allowed me to believe so completely that we were meant to be together. The sacrament of marriage is sacred, and, watching our wedding video, I can see how serious I was in those moments. I was taking in every word, every commitment, every prayer for our lasting love. And that day, I thought John was too.

My uncle married us, so I had the opportunity to talk to him about what I wanted to include in our wedding—the readings, the music, and all of the people who would play important roles that day. One verse I knew I wanted to include was the classic description of love from the New Testament.

> *"Love is patient, love is kind. It does not envy, it does not boast, it is not proud. It is not rude, it is*

> *not self-seeking, it is not easily angered, it keeps no record of wrongs. Love does not delight in evil but rejoices with the truth. It always protects, always trusts, always hopes, always perseveres. Love never fails." (1 Corinthians 13:4–7, NIV)*

There's a reason so many couples choose to include this reading in their wedding. It says it all. It covers everything you need to know about being a good partner: patience, kindness, humility, and truth. I looked back on the years that John and I had been together and I saw all of that in him, in us, and in the marriage we were embarking on that day.

During the homily, when my uncle spoke to our family and friends about the scripture reading, he specifically talked about the "reality" of love. Today that has such a different meaning for my marriage to John. For me, and likely for everyone in the church except John, the reality of love inspires reflection on how hard marriage can be sometimes. When you commit to being with someone for better or worse, you don't know what you are in for, but you promise to stick with it.

Now, knowing so much more than I knew at the time, John's actions look different to me, and I wonder what must have been going through his head during the ceremony. Was he thinking that the reality of love meant that I'd never question him or any of his actions? That now I'd never be able to leave him? That my convictions were so strong that he could get away with almost anything and I would stay committed to our marriage? On our wedding day, I saw John's fidgeting and nervous smirk as a mirror of my own excitement for our big day. Now I see those same gestures and sense that even then he was planning, calculating, keeping all of his stories straight. After all, we still had our reception to get through. He had to be wondering what the rest of the day would bring.

John and me on our wedding day.

It started sweetly with the last-minute best man, Phil, saying in his toast that, if you asked John's friends about his engagement to Tonia, they'd be completely shocked and baffled. Everyone in the room chuckled a little nervously, unsure of where his story was going. He went on to say that he and John were skeptical people, and that was part of why they got along so well. He concluded by saying, "To see John truly be in love is an inspiring thing for me and probably for his friends too."

It was a nice moment, and it wasn't the only one. Our wedding reception was a beautiful celebration, with family and friends sharing their best wishes. We cut our cake, had our first dance as a married couple, and invited the rest of our guests to join us on the dance floor.

A few weeks after we were married, when John had already returned to California, I got a copy of our wedding tape from the videographer. I couldn't wait to see it and settled in to watch how the day started, the ceremony, and highlights of the reception. It's amazing how much you don't see or don't remember on the most important days of your life. For most people, being able to watch their wedding video means remembering the most touching moments of the day, seeing parts of the ceremony or reception from a different angle, and hearing kind words for you and your partner directly from your wedding guests. John and I had that, and I enjoyed seeing our day played back again, but there was one part at the end of the video that struck me—of the groomsmen, clearly at the end of the night.

"We're here to celebrate John," one of them shouted into the microphone, his speech slurred.

Another groomsman chimed in with, "We won't tell you what his other nickname was when we knew him, prior to his being married."

Another groomsman shouted, "Filthy John!"

The small group of groomsmen wouldn't let it drop.

"And how did he get a name like *Filthy*?" The camera wobbled, panned left and right, but none of the groomsmen would answer. Giving up, they took the camera and microphone to other guests, but the same groomsmen would be back again.

Mixed in with stories about how people knew John and me were other strange comments. One groomsman was asked about his "Cincinnati trips" with John, which caused the group to burst into knowing laughter and the nickname—"Filthy" John Meehan—to surface again.

"Let me start by saying this: John Meehan's nickname is Filthy John Meehan."

A chorus of "whys" and mock surprise came from the others, muddled by the sounds of the reception and the drunk men talking over one another. One of them asked, "Do you remember how he first got that nickname?"

John then appeared in the video, relaxed and laughing with his friend. The groomsman continued, "Yes, I do, but it cannot be divulged on camera."

Through more muddled laughter, one of the groomsmen shouted, "They should have called him 'the cruiser,'" before the film cut back to the wedding reception.

John wasn't showing even a little concern during the conversation. He was laughing with them, just like I had seen him joking around all night. There wasn't any part of me that was overly concerned about what they were saying—mostly, I think, because they just looked like a bunch of drunk frat brothers at the end of a night out together. The audio was a little muffled and they were hard to understand, but I still asked John about it the next time we talked.

"What were they talking about, calling you 'Filthy'?" I'd ask him.

"It means nothing," he told me. "They were just drunk."

Having just watched the video, I couldn't deny that. Everyone had a wonderful time, plenty to drink, and as far as I knew, John and I had started our lives together with a wedding none of us would soon forget. I didn't anticipate at the time that anyone would ever watch clips of our wedding reception on the TV show *Dateline*, but that was just one of many surprises I would experience in the years to come.

CHAPTER 6

STARTING A FAMILY

Mom, I just got a direct message from somebody who thinks he could be my half-brother.

—ABBY MEEHAN

John and I living apart for much of our dating relationship made it far easier for him to create and maintain the image of himself that he wanted me to know and love. When I moved to Cincinnati for school early in our relationship, he stayed in Dayton, but we saw each other often, making our time together on weekends and holidays that much more special. And when I was completing my last year of CRNA school, he was attending law school in California. That was a much greater distance, but we were young and focused on completing our education so that we'd be set up for successful careers the rest of our lives. It was hard sometimes, but it was temporary and didn't seem like more than we could handle. And being apart for a short time was worth it for us to both make huge strides toward our professional goals.

I'd eventually learn that while we were in a relationship but living apart, John was dating other women. The distance made this a lot easier for him to get away with, both because I wasn't around to ask questions and because he didn't have to tell as many people about me. When I'd visit, I'd meet some of his friends, but as far as women he met at work or in class, it was easy for John to say he was single and never have anyone doubt him.

Around December of 1989, when John was still in Dayton and I was in Cincinnati, one of the women he had been seeing, Yvette, told John she was pregnant. The two hadn't been together for that long, and Yvette told John that she felt it was best that they terminate the pregnancy. John agreed to pick her up and take her to the abortion clinic, but he never showed up. They rescheduled for another time, and again he didn't show up. John left Dayton and the two would never speak again.

By 1990, while I was planning our wedding and attending a rigorous nurse anesthesia program in Ohio, John was living, working, and going to school in California, and we had settled into a comfortable long-distance relationship. Right after we were married, John had to return to California, and I went right back to school in Cincinnati. Our wedding had been beautiful, but we were quickly thrown back into our busy lives.

After I graduated as a nurse anesthetist in February of 1991, I moved to California to live with John. It was the logical choice because it was easy enough as a CRNA for me to find a good job, and I was so glad we'd finally be living in the same state again and in the same house full time for the first time in our relationship. But once we weren't separated by geography, we still weren't together as much as I thought we'd be. I quickly realized just how lonely I was.

I had a stressful new job as a CRNA at San Bernardino County Medical Center and spent evenings and weekends studying for my certification exam. John was busy working as a law clerk during the day and taking classes at night, so I was alone a lot. And while I had made new friends in California, it just wasn't the same as the community I had come from in Ohio.

At the end of 1991, after we had been married for about a year and mostly living in California, to the best of my knowledge John was doing well as a law clerk and, as he had in his undergraduate studies, was excelling in law school. I was honest with him about how I was feeling and hopeful that we could find a solution to get us through the next year.

In my mind, there were small things that we could change that would help a lot. One that I vividly remember is how often he'd play basketball with friends, as often as a few times a week. Exercise is important, I wanted him to have ways to blow off steam with friends, and I tried to remind myself that he was used to living alone, even though we were in a relationship. I thought when I told him how I was feeling, he'd offer to spend less time with friends or come up with another way for us to make time for each other more often.

Instead, John suggested we move back to Ohio. He said he could reenroll in the University of Dayton School of Law and continue his education there, allowing me to be closer to friends and family. He even mentioned that he didn't want to raise kids in California, so we'd have to move eventually. Why not now?

I was moved by his willingness to return to Ohio just to make sure I was happy. As far as I knew, John had heard me describe how I was feeling and found a solution. There would be minimal disruption to our life plan and ultimately we'd be happier. My concerns came at a very convenient time for him, and he knew just how to flip the situation to his advantage.

At the end of 1991, we returned to Ohio. I quickly found a job and John met with the University of Dayton about reenrolling—or at least he told me he did, and that they had told him he'd need to wait a full year to start classes. What I didn't know at the time was that John's roommates from his first round at UD believed that John had actually been struggling to keep up with his coursework and had failed his last semester of classes. I suppose I won't ever really know the truth, but I suspect he was denied admittance and just told me a lie to support the new narrative he was building.

John told me he didn't think he even wanted to be a lawyer anymore. He wanted to be a nurse anesthetist—just like me.

I was shocked. I listened as he shared that he didn't think working in the legal field was the right path for him. He said he didn't think being an attorney would be fulfilling. In fact, it was watching me over the years that helped him realize just what a fulfilling career could look like.

When he shared this, I was supportive, but I have to admit that I was a little disappointed. He was well into law school, and a career change like this meant he would have to go back to school to complete a second undergraduate degree and then try to get into a nurse anesthesia program. He had been so close to graduating and working in his field as an attorney, I didn't fully understand why he'd want to quit at this point. But I also didn't want him to be unhappy and I understood what it felt like to be called to work in the medical field. And I thought he had just been willing to move for my happiness, so of course I was open to changes that would make him happy.

So instead of finishing law school in Ohio, John enrolled in classes to complete a second bachelor's degree that would prepare him for nurse anesthesia school. In some ways, it felt like a step backward, but I had started my career as a CRNA, so we were moving toward financial stability, even with John still in school. And we were living together, near my friends and family, so our lives in general were good.

For the first few years, we had what I thought was a pretty normal marriage. We had ups and downs—like the phone call from the woman who claimed she and John had slept together the night before. We had sad times too, like when my grandmother passed away. John also had a significant issue with his health.

In 1994, when John was approaching the end of his bachelor's degree in nursing, he had a serious bout of kidney stones. Working in medicine, I have learned that medical emergencies often come at what seems like the worst time, but they can also have transformative effects. Thinking about the timing, I believe John's painful kidney stones and extensive recovery contributed to two significant turning points in our lives.

His kidney stones were so severe that he needed a painful procedure called a nephrostomy. An interventional radiologist placed a tube in John's side connected to his kidney, allowing urine to drain directly from his kidney into a bag outside of his body. The procedure was traumatizing enough, but John had continuous complications. We were in and out of the ER multiple times over the weeks it took him to recover.

Knowing now that John had experimented with drugs in his younger years, I often wonder if this is when his addiction really kicked into overdrive. I didn't know it when I met him, but he had been a casual user of cocaine. Nothing in the police reports that I've read or in the conversations I've had with his friends from that time in his life indicates to me that he was an addict at this point in his life. In fact, it seems very clear that buying and selling cocaine was a lucrative business for him and a way for him to make money off the addictions of others. Using at that time would have been counterproductive to his goal of making money.

John's exposure to narcotics for his nephrostomy could have been what triggered his drug addiction, taking him from a recreational drug user to a full-blown addict. Treatment of a legitimate ailment is a common way people in and outside of the medical profession become addicted. I now believe that at least a few of our visits to the emergency room were the result of John's drug-seeking behaviors. The addiction John developed had its roots in a real medical event, and John knew enough about the medical field to fool everyone—ER doctors, his urologist, and even his wife. He was the perfect candidate to go from patient to addict without anyone noticing.

Amid managing John's medical care, I wasn't thinking that he may be developing an addiction. I was seeing his surgical wound, hearing the pain in his voice, and feeling the frustration that so many patients and their loved ones experience when an already difficult procedure doesn't go as well as planned. His pain dragged on, and I felt terrible for him. Only now do I wonder how much of it was real.

One day during all this chaos, I was with John in the hospital. I had just helped him manage the tube in his side and a Foley catheter so that he would be able to complete the simple but now much more appreciated task of taking a shower. Out of the blue, he looked at me and said, "I think we should start trying to have a baby."

I was shocked that John chose that moment to say we should have a baby. And I was pretty sure that it would be impossible in his present condition. Watching John suffer, I was focused on helping him heal. We had been talking about having a family, but I wanted to be sure that he was ready and that it wasn't just his recent struggles talking. As some time passed, if I had any real concerns, they disappeared. I knew we were taking the next, amazing step in our lives together. I also knew that I was going to do everything I possibly could to make sure that we were successful. I had been raised in a wonderful, loving home with my sister and our two parents who cared deeply for us, providing us with all of the love and security we needed.

I always knew I wanted to create a loving home for children of my own, and I thought John, who hadn't had a happy childhood, felt the same way. But each time I brought up the idea, he would tell me the timing wasn't right and that we should wait—there was always a reason. And honestly, with him in school, I knew he was right.

I felt confident we'd have kids one day, and I was anxious for that day to come, but I wanted John to be ready too. I did small things, like buying an amazing secondhand crib for the baby we'd have someday, and I'd ask John what timeframe he thought we needed. But otherwise, I tried to ignore the ticking of my biological clock and give John the time he needed. The day he told me that he was ready was one I will never forget.

I was twenty-nine years old when we decided to get pregnant, so I worried there was a chance we'd have a little trouble making it happen. But I was going to use every resource available to me, and one of those resources was a fertility doctor I frequently worked with. He told me to get an ovulation test kit and track my cycle more closely, so that John and I would know our best opportunity to get pregnant. Testing and tracking? I am a planner, so this was right up my alley.

But I didn't need my planning skills for very long. I was pregnant the very first month. I can't even describe how ecstatic I was. And I loved being pregnant. I bought diapers midway through my pregnancy just to smell that smell. And as close as my family already was, the baby brought us even closer.

I remember designing the nursery with help from my dad. Sponge painting was all the rage at that time, and I painstakingly squished a sponge all around the bottom of the nursery walls while my dad hung wallpaper on the top half to complement my work. With great care, we put together the crib and brought in a dresser. I remember carefully selecting a Beatrix Potter mobile, so characters from the world of Peter Rabbit would spin for the baby's entertainment.

About six weeks into my pregnancy, I started to experience significant episodes of nausea. It wasn't easy, but I muscled through and never missed a day of work. As happy as I was, I always had this nagging feeling that someday something big and terrible would happen. My life just seemed too blessed. While I was pregnant, I worried constantly that since all of my friends already had beautiful, healthy babies, maybe my baby wouldn't be healthy. As irrational as it sounds, it felt real, and working in medicine didn't help. Each ultrasound put my fears to rest, but it wouldn't be long before that sensation that something was off would return.

I also remembered that John had made comments to me about a prior girlfriend he had broken up with because she gained twenty pounds. This had come up years earlier, and he hadn't said it to me as any kind of a threat. It was just a passing comment about a girl he had once dated. But in my anxious state that memory returned to me, and I worried that the weight I'd gain with the baby would make John find me unattractive. It was a thought in the back of my head, but I stayed focused on doing everything possible to grow a healthy baby.

In February of that year, when I was about six months pregnant, I celebrated my thirtieth birthday. John and I couldn't celebrate together, but because of the unusual living arrangement we had for most of our marriage, that wasn't a big deal. We had learned to celebrate each other, our holidays and our successes, on our own timeline. We wouldn't be together on my birthday, but we made plans to celebrate the next week.

The actual week of my birthday, John had a break in his schedule and took the opportunity, as he often did, to make a last-minute trip to visit friends and his younger half-brother out of state. He told me that he'd be in California, visiting his brother Michael, old friends, and a few college professors, while I was at home, keeping up my regular work schedule.

Years later I would learn that John had traveled all the way to California, but it wasn't to see old friends. He had arranged to meet Kathy, a woman he had met when he was a law clerk in California. The two had worked together but hadn't been romantically involved. They stayed in touch after John left the firm to move to Ohio, and eventually he told Kathy that he and I were separated. Of course we weren't, but Kathy knew he had gotten married. When he pursued her romantically, he needed a way to explain why he was so suddenly single.

After John and I really did separate, I learned from Kathy that she had her suspicions that John was still married. She recalled a time when the two of them were at a swap meet together, and John was fascinated by a small pink suitcase, clearly designed for a child. Since, to the best of her knowledge, John didn't have any children, she thought his interest was strange.

"Is there something you want to tell me?" she remembers asking him in that moment.

His too-quick reply was "No," and that he just "hadn't seen anything like those small suitcases before." Though Kathy found it odd, it was just a small blip on her radar. After that trip, Kathy and John's romantic relationship faded, but they stayed in contact for years. John even emailed her a few days before he died. He made an ominous comment—that he wanted her to tell his kids that he loved them. At the time Kathy had no way of knowing what that comment meant and that John would be dead in just a few days.

When John returned from his trip to California, he brought me a beautiful pair of diamond earrings for my birthday. I was stunned. It was such a wonderfully unexpected gift, since we never really exchanged lavish birthday presents and because we were so focused on getting ready for the baby. Because I was completely unaware of why he had really been in California, that moment in time felt perfect. I was pregnant with our first child, and my husband was doting on me, spoiling me on my birthday.

It's strange to think of those days now. I can't help but wonder what John had been thinking and what his motivation could have been for bringing me those earrings. I hadn't been upset with him. I'd been busy with work and focused on the baby. I have learned over the years that psychopaths don't feel guilty, so I know he didn't buy them because he felt badly about the affair. It leaves me with a single conclusion—that moment that was so special to me was just another calculated manipulation on his part. He was playing the part of a loving husband without having any genuine feelings at all.

I may have also been distracted by all of the other incredible things happening in my life. One of my friends from work threw me the biggest baby shower I had ever been to. Like they had at our wedding, friends and family shared sentiments of love, support, and excitement for the baby who would be joining our family in just a few months.

In June of 1995, our baby girl was born. Happy, healthy, and everything I could have asked for, she was the perfect baby. Or maybe it is more accurate to say she was a very typical baby. She was of course challenging at times. But I loved every minute of being a mother. I knew from the start how blessed I was that our family had grown to include such a precious child.

When John and I finally got to meet our sweet angel, we had to choose a name. Though we had quite a few different ideas, John really loved the name Emily. I thought it was sweet that he cared so much, and I liked the name, too. So we agreed—sharing my middle name with the baby, we were ready to introduce Emily Ann Meehan to the world.

Like most new parents, John and I were quickly swept up into our new routine. Emily's first weeks flew by, probably because John and I were sleep-deprived, like most new parents, but also because the full life we were leading didn't slow down just because we had added a new baby to our home. Before I knew it, my maternity leave was up, and I was getting ready to go back to work.

John holding Emily.

The change was bittersweet. I loved being a nurse anesthetist and felt so fortunate to do work every day that was so rewarding. But once I had Emily, I also wanted to spend every hour of every day with her. I know my story isn't unusual, and people had warned me how hard it would be to go back to work, even work that I loved. But until you experience it, you just don't realize how consuming the love for your children is.

I assumed John was right there with me, feeling the same pull between his career in medicine and family life. People often wonder what kind of a dad he was when they hear about all of the horrible things he did. They know him as a con artist, a drug addict, and a liar. And it's true. He was all of those things. But he was also very involved with taking care of Emily.

His attentiveness to her, his willingness to change her diapers, and his interest in playing with her as she grew up helped cover up all of the dark secrets he was hiding. He was a nurse, so caring for Emily was a skill he had learned in school and practiced in his work. He didn't resist spending time with Emily either—kids were safe for him to be around. I suspect he could relax around them in a way that he couldn't with adults. Little kids aren't going to out a con artist.

We had plenty of support when we were living in Ohio. My parents, even though they still worked, would visit and take care of Emily as much as they could. But the biggest gift we had as a working family was a wonderful neighbor across the street, Miss Terri, who had a family of her own. She took care of Emily when I was at work. Her home was a loving, safe environment. Short of caring for her myself, I couldn't have asked for a better place for Emily to spend her days.

Later that year, John was accepted to Middle Tennessee School of Anesthesia. This was an incredible opportunity for him, but if Emily and I stayed in Ohio and he went to Tennessee, the distance would be too great to manage.

We made the tough decision to relocate, away from our supportive neighbors and my family. I found another great job in Tennessee, and I worked as our family's sole supporter and cared for Emily while John was in school. It was a big change for our little family, but unbeknownst to me there had been even bigger changes in John's life that I'm not sure he even knew about. I would learn years later that Yvette, the pregnant girlfriend John had abandoned, had changed her mind about the baby. Before Emily was born, before we were even married, John had become a father to a baby boy.

CHAPTER 7

CRACKS ON THE SURFACE

After Christmas, we need to talk.

—JOHN TO TONIA, DECEMBER 1999

As a new family of three, with John's graduation from Middle Tennessee School of Anesthesia fast approaching, we talked about what the next chapter of our lives would look like. One of our early plans was to move to Florida—warm weather and job opportunities for both of us made it an appealing option. My parents had even agreed to follow us when they retired, keeping our extended family together. They were as fooled by John's charisma as I was and had no idea that anything was wrong with their daughter's marriage.

Ultimately it was that same commitment to family that kept us all from relocating to the Sunshine State. My paternal grandmother was living in a long-term care facility in Ohio, and even though she usually didn't even know who my dad was, he and my mom just couldn't leave her. This reality opened us up to the idea of moving back to Ohio. A classmate of John's had a sister in the Dayton area and he told us how great the job market was in Ohio. We decided to check it out.

After researching the market, applying at a few different hospitals, and interviewing, John and I decided that Dayton would be the best place for us. In fact, we both ended up at Miami Valley Hospital—the hospital I had left just two years prior. We were in a new and exciting place in our lives now. We were about to be a two-income household, and as CRNAs, we were able to choose a really nice home for our little family of three.

We ultimately chose a beautiful home in a neighborhood just outside of Sycamore Creek Country Club in Springboro, Ohio. We were in a cul-de-sac—a dream location for any parent. There was no traffic and plenty of space for kids to play safely.

By the time John graduated, we had already settled into our new house. He had done his last clinical rotation in Ohio, so we actually had to travel back to Tennessee for his graduation ceremony. But I was glad to do it—even with a toddler. Completing this level of education and beginning his career as a nurse anesthetist, as I had a few years earlier, was something to be celebrated.

Middle Tennessee School of Anesthesia had an amazing tradition for all of its students. When graduates walked across the stage to receive their diplomas, the officiant would read a statement of thanks submitted by the student in advance. I felt emotional hearing these heartfelt messages shared, even for many people I didn't even know. I was sure that moving our family, working full-time to support him while he was in school, and being Emily's primary care provider would result in my own heartfelt thank-you from John. Instead, I heard something like an honorable mention: "Thanks to my wife, Tonia, for her support."

But what wife hasn't felt a little disappointed by her husband at some point, right? I didn't let it ruin our day, and I excitedly continued the celebration of all that John had accomplished. At the time, I don't think I even really thought of it as more than inconsiderate. Now, after learning how calculated John was in all of his relationships, I see that lackluster thank-you in a different light. He didn't feel any level of genuine appreciation for how I had supported our family through the previous challenging years, and this was just the first time I had really heard evidence of that out loud.

John and me at his graduation from Middle Tennessee School of Anesthesia in 1998.

In our new home, I quickly became friends with our new neighbors. I was pleasantly surprised to discover that one of them was a childhood friend of mine. It was an incredible coincidence that I couldn't see as anything but a good sign that we were in the perfect place to raise our family. With my parents close by and friendly neighbors with young kids Emily could play with, I felt so content.

I remember standing in the kitchen one day, talking to John, who had sprawled out on the couch after a long day of work. It was an average day, but for some reason it's stuck in my memory all these years later. I was thinking about all of the schooling we had completed, how hard we had worked to achieve the excellent jobs we had, and the fact that we were talking about having another baby. Overwhelmed with gratitude, I said to John, "The next ten years are going to be some of the best of our lives."

His flat reply was, "What was wrong with the last ten years?"

His comment left an odd heaviness in the air. For starters, the last ten years had been hard, especially the last two. I guess he didn't feel the same way that I did. And knowing that psychopaths don't plan for the future or even think past the current moment, I suppose it makes sense that he didn't share the wonderment I felt about our life.

Despite these little moments that now flicker in my memory as clues to how John was really feeling, we decided to continue growing our family. Organized as I am, once we agreed to try for baby number two, I got an ovulation test kit and made a plan. And even though I probably would have made a plan anyway, this time we were working around a new challenge.

John had graduated as a nurse anesthetist, but he hadn't taken his boards yet. In some states, you used to be able to work as a graduate nurse anesthetist while you studied for your boards, and in other states you couldn't—you'd have to pass your exam before you could be employed in the field. Ohio was one of the states where you had to complete your exam first. But we were lucky—an anesthesiologist friend of ours, Dr. Bob, had a need for an anesthetist at his hospital in Michigan, a state with medical facilities that would hire you while you were studying for your exam. It would mean we'd be apart for days at a time when John was working, but it wouldn't be as challenging as the schedule we had made work before, and this was an incredible opportunity for him and our family.

Of course, John thought this was an excellent idea. At the time I assumed that he saw the opportunity like I did as one that would benefit our family. Now I'm sure he actually saw it as a chance to operate with more freedom, since the physical distance between us would make it easier for him to live his life however he wanted. And I would soon learn that he did just that.

In January of 1999, I was able to attend a continuing education conference in St. Thomas, so John, Emily, and I turned it into an amazing Caribbean vacation. The day before we returned home, I noticed some breast tenderness and, suspicious that I was already pregnant, asked John to stop at a drug store on our way home from the airport.

When we got home, John was still bringing in our suitcases, but I just couldn't wait. I ran upstairs to take the test. Sure enough, I was pregnant.

Still light and happy from our vacation, this news put me over the top. John had come up the stairs, and I ran to him with a big smile on my face. I showed him the stick and waited for his reaction. Everything we had talked about and planned for was coming together.

"Congratulations," he said and gave me a small smile.

I was confused by his response, and this time, I really didn't have a good way to explain it away. *We* were to be congratulated, not just me. We had decided together to have another baby. We had talked about what that would take and what that would mean. Why was his response so one-sided? We had just shared an incredible vacation with Emily, and I simply couldn't understand why he wasn't more excited.

In the following months I'd learn that John had started a relationship with a woman he worked with in Michigan. While we were planning family vacations and talking about having another baby, he was carrying on a serious relationship with a doctor who thought John and I were divorcing. He had to tell her about us eventually because he had to explain why he kept returning to Ohio, but for months he had told her that it was Emily he went to see—certainly not his pregnant wife.

While I was pregnant with our second baby, I could feel a growing distance in our marriage, but it was hard to explain. I knew it was there. I knew I wasn't imagining it. I didn't have nearly the amount of information I have today, so I was mostly confused and worried about what was happening. But I was also working full-time and pregnant, so I had plenty of distractions.

I worked right up until the day of my delivery, just like I had with Emily, so that I could have as much time off as possible after the baby was born. My obstetrician asked if we wanted to induce the week before the planned date, but after discussing it with John, we decided to wait. I was excited to have our new baby, but I was also okay waiting. John's rationale was different. He said it didn't work out well in his schedule for the baby to be early, and after all, what's the hurry? Clearly he had never been pregnant for nine months.

That September morning, John had worked the night before. He didn't get off until 7:00 a.m., so I packed everything I needed and drove myself to Miami Valley Hospital in Dayton. The plan was for John to meet me at the hospital after his shift. I bumped into another CRNA in the parking garage, and she saw me nine months pregnant and struggling to carry everything I had brought. She, not my husband, was there to help me that morning.

Abigail Mae Meehan was born the afternoon of September 13, 1999. The delivery was uncomplicated, and both John and my mom were there when Abby came into the world. Because John had worked the night before, he was tired and had been sleeping in one of the call rooms when it came time to push, but he did make it for the big moment.

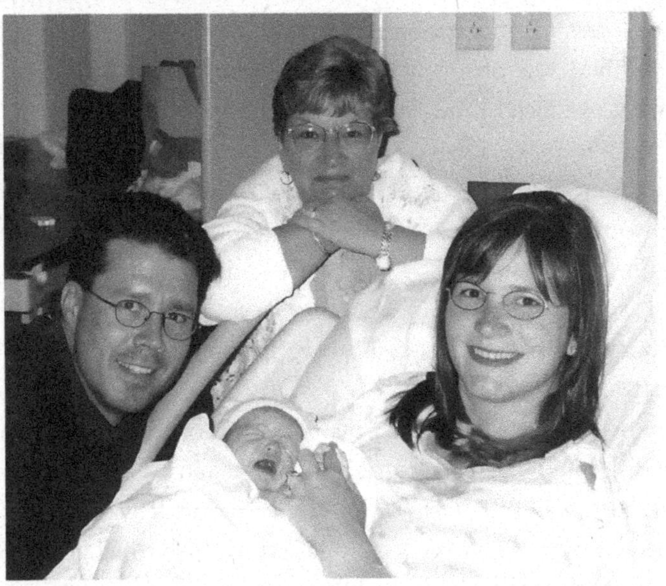

John, my mom, and me with Abby the day she was born.

And it wasn't long before little Emily got to meet her sister. My dad went and picked her up from childcare so that she could come to the hospital with the rest of the family. She was thrilled to meet the newest addition to our family.

We all watched as Emily patted Abby's head and sang her a little song. My heart swelled—even our nurse teared up at the sweetness of the moment. How could she not be moved by the immediate devotion of sisterly love we all had the pleasure of witnessing? At that time, I had no idea that John felt nothing in that moment.

The second night I was in the hospital with Abby, John brought Emily back to visit and let me know that he was going to play racquetball with a friend of his who was a doctor at the hospital. Disappointed, I said okay and turned my attention to the girls.

Emily was over the moon. She wanted to do everything for the new little baby. That night, Emily fed Abby a bottle and helped change her diaper. She was beaming with excitement at her new sister. I knew then that I was witnessing the beginning of a relationship that would be crucial for both of them for the rest of their lives. Even though I could feel John's absence that evening, I felt their love more. And I'm so grateful they've had each other, because I can't imagine either of them going through what our family endured without the other.

John was gone much longer than I thought he'd be, especially considering Abby was just over a day old. Eventually, our labor and delivery nurse told me that Emily couldn't stay the night, so John took her home. I was sad to see them leave, but I knew it wouldn't be long before we were all together again.

Returning home with Abby, we settled into our new busy routine—the kind of joyful and exhausted busy that comes with adding a new baby to a family. After a few days, John had already begun working a few shifts in Michigan again. I was surrounded by so many friends and family members that I barely noticed his absence. And when he was home, he was so attentive to Abby, it was easy to ignore any concerns that crept into my mind.

The holidays were fast approaching, and on the day before Christmas Eve, I waited with the girls for John to come home from his job in Michigan. I needed him to watch them while I did some last-minute shopping. We were expecting him early in the day, but hours passed and he didn't arrive. Finally, after not returning any of the messages I had left for him all day, he showed up.

Upset that he was so late without even having the courtesy to call, I said, "John, is your phone broken?" My snarky tone did not go unnoticed. He responded defensively, saying that I was the one making this situation difficult. He said ominously that, after the holiday, we needed to have a talk. I didn't really understand at the time why we couldn't just talk then, but it's clear to me now that he was already plotting to leave our family, and I had just handed him his way out.

Over the holiday, I thought about how I had responded to him and believed, even if not wholeheartedly, that maybe I had been too hard on him. Maybe the stress of the new baby, us living apart, and still keeping up with the job I loved so much was taking a toll on our marriage. Maybe I could do better.

Christmas came and went, and John still wouldn't talk to me about what was going on. I pushed for the conversation and finally he gave in, telling me that he just wasn't happy. I had to admit that I wasn't happy either, but it didn't feel like anything we couldn't fix. We agreed that we needed help. I wanted us to be happy again, so marriage counseling was a step I was glad to take. And even though the conversation we had was stressful and even scary, I knew it was necessary. I never thought marriage would be easy, and we were nearly ten years in with two children. Cracks at this point were normal.

A few months later—after meetings with two different counselors, because John didn't like the first one—I came home to find a large, official-looking envelope addressed to John in our mailbox. I saw that the return address was a law office, and my heart started racing. I knew exactly what it was, and I couldn't resist opening it. I felt sick and panicked when I saw the contents.

John had filed for divorce.

CHAPTER 8

TILL DEATH DO US PART (OR UNTIL YOU CHANGE YOUR MIND)

The court further finds from the evidence adduced that the parties are incompatible, that by reason thereof, and they are entitled to a divorce.

—TONIA AND JOHN'S DIVORCE DECREE, DECEMBER 31, 2001

When I learned that John had filed for divorce, I was stunned—not only because I didn't know what had changed between us, but also because I always believed that no matter how bad things got, John and I would work through it. I knew we would have hard times like every married couple, but one of the things I loved about John was that I believed he was as committed to the sanctity of marriage as I was. I now realize that, throughout our entire marriage,

John simply mirrored what he discovered was important to me. I saw him as my loving life partner, so I was an open book. That gave him powerful ammunition, and our separation was when I really started to see who I had married.

Like many divorce cases and custody battles, my separation from John took months, and the custody battle for Emily and Abby took years. This surprises some people for a few reasons.

A common question is, "But he was such a terrible person—using and selling drugs, associated with various crimes, leaving you threatening messages. Didn't that give you a ton of evidence against him?" The short answer is no, but I'm reminded of the long answer when I read through my journal from that time. Like the rest of the world, today I know John as a psychopath—he always was one. But it wasn't until our divorce and custody battle that all of those pieces began to be revealed. I didn't have a mountain of evidence. I had tiny pieces of a terrifying picture slowly coming together. I felt like a lot of people I encountered thought what I was saying was an exaggeration. Some people seemed to view me as just an angry ex-wife whose husband left her for another woman. It may have seemed to them that I was conjuring up all kinds of stories to get even.

It's also important to remember that, as a lifelong con artist, John was skilled at lying. A lot of his lies would eventually be uncovered, but while we were separating, I still only knew some of the truth he was hiding. There are things that happened then that I only now fully understand because it took years for critical pieces of John's stories to fall apart.

Another common question I hear is, "If John really was a psychopath, why would he drag out the divorce and custody battle? Don't psychopaths operate without making connections to other people—even family—making them uninterested in maintaining relationships?" That is a great point, and it is important for anyone engaging with a true psychopath to remember. But it's also important to remember that psychopaths look for opportunities they can manipulate to their advantage. Dr. Christine Marie Cocchiola, a clinician who specializes in family trauma, wrote the perfect explanation of this at a high level in the book she coauthored, *Framed: Women in the Family Court Underworld*, based on her experience working with women attempting to separate from abusers.

> *Their partners are bent on revenge, control, and power at any cost. They are coercive controllers/narcissistic abusers—and their campaign can take the form of psychological abuse such as gaslighting, manipulation, intimidation, and isolation, financial abuse, legal abuse, and of course their favorite tactic, the weaponization of the children.*

When John and I were in court, he was still trying to keep himself out of trouble, get as much money as possible, and maintain his reputation in the medical profession, but his primary focus was revenge—he wanted to destroy me.

It's been decades since John and I spent years fighting in and out of court, and I'm not sure I would even remember the details if not for the journals I kept at the time. Like little time capsules, even the simplest dated notes I created take me back to those days in an instant, reminding me how often I was scared and confused, but also determined to win my fight for the life Emily, Abby, and I deserved.

I do remember that in April of 2000, when we were in counseling, it never felt like John ever really engaged. As he had done in the past, John planned a last-minute trip out west to visit someone—I can't remember who. When he came back home, he worked for a couple of nights in Dayton and then left to work in Michigan. He left his suitcase open and unpacked on the bedroom floor, and eventually I got sick of looking at it. Since I was doing laundry, I decided to unpack it myself, not expecting to find anything other than dirty clothes. Instead, I discovered a small plastic bag, like something a gift card would be in. I looked inside and found an empty syringe.

I couldn't imagine why he would have this in his suitcase. Being in the medical profession, I knew I could pull back on the plunger to see if anything had ever been in the syringe. Sure enough, I could see that the inside was still wet from whatever substance had been in it. My head was spinning with possibilities, all of them bad. I decided at that moment to keep the syringe, hide it, and see if John mentioned anything when he came home and found the suitcase unpacked.

Inconsistencies from our more than ten years together were now all bubbling up in my mind. Was John using drugs? Was he having an affair? If John wasn't going to tell me, then I would have to go snooping to figure it out.

I went downstairs to the office that John had set up in the basement bedroom of our house. I didn't know what I was looking for exactly, so I just started looking through everything. I searched the desk first and didn't find anything interesting. I didn't know any of his passwords, so the computer was of no help. I did come across the cap to a medication vial and a capped needle—two more pieces to the puzzle that would be hard for him to explain.

I opened the closet doors and started examining everything inside. I soon found a notepad with directions to a hotel in Knoxville, Tennessee, in a woman's handwriting. My stomach turned. I also found a photo of residents at a medical center where John was working, with one woman's picture circled.

The top shelf was high, so I pulled a chair over so I could see the entire shelf. Pushed all the way to the back was a red cedar box. I pulled the box out, opened it, and to my dismay I saw it was filled with anesthesia drugs—vials of Versed and fentanyl.

What the hell? Why are these here?

John's stash of diverted anesthesia drugs I found in his office.

Never once in my career have I accidentally brought home controlled substances. There was no innocent explanation for this. It had to be intentional drug diversion. My heart was racing. I put the drug box back exactly as I had found it.

John never mentioned the syringe in his suitcase and I didn't mention finding it or the box of drugs. From time to time I would check the box to see if maybe John had just stashed the drugs in the closet and forgotten about them. But the inventory had changed every time I checked. He was frequently accessing the drugs in the box.

I confided in Dr. Bob and he instructed me on how to have the syringe contents tested. The results came back positive for benzodiazepines and opiates. I eventually asked John about the syringe I had found, and he, of course, lied, saying it had lidocaine in it so he could numb up and lance a cyst. He must have seen on my face that I knew he was making that up. His tone and demeanor changed.

"What do you think I'm doing, Tonia?"

"Nothing," I said. "I just want you to know that if you have a problem I will help you."

"Well, I don't," he replied and stormed off.

What neither of us knew in that moment was that the eventual help I would provide would mean he would lose his license to practice as a nurse anesthetist. I had helped John become a member of this high-achieving and respected profession and I would soon be compelled to make sure he lost that privilege.

In July of 2000, a few months into our separation, my attorney advised me to begin keeping a journal. She even advised me not to call it a diary, as that would make it discoverable and John's attorney could request it through a subpoena. I went back about a month and started recording all the events and details I could remember and that I thought were important. Reading them decades later, I'm reminded of how I was feeling as the months rolled by. Important updates, critical to our divorce proceedings and custody battle, are mixed with everyday information like the girls' Christmas pageants and card games with friends.

> *Thursday, June 8, 2000 (recorded on July 7)*
>
> *11:00 appointment with counselor. It was decided that John would find a place to live. He told me that he would pay all the bills for the house and that I could stay in the house as long as I wanted. He said he didn't want us to have to move. I told him that I would want the extra support over and above the child support in writing. He refused and said that I would just have to trust him.*
>
> *Thursday, June 15, 2000 (recorded on July 7)*
>
> *11:00 appointment with counselor (Dr. Wilbert). We again agreed that the living arrangements needed to change because it was not healthy for us to be under the same roof. John stated that he would be out by the weekend after we celebrated Emily's birthday.*
>
> *Sunday, June 18, 2000 (recorded on July 7)*
>
> *John's last night at 25 Colonial Way. He took Emily to camp at MVS on Monday morning. Said he was going to stay in his call room until he found a place.*
>
> *Friday, June 23, 2000 (recorded on July 7)*
>
> *John left letters on kitchen counter dated 6/23. He worked 7:00 pm on Friday to about 5 pm*

on Sunday. Then drove to Michigan and worked M-F. Came home Saturday afternoon July 1 and took Emily for a few hours. Did not call to talk to Emily for 8 days. Could have called while I was working.

Thursday, June 29 (recorded on July 7)

4 pm Dad took me to meet with Gianaglou [sic] (lawyer) who advised me not to sign anything and referred me to an attorney in Lebanon.

Saturday, July 1

John called at 9:45 am and requested to have Emily for the afternoon. I told him that I had had $26.00 in my checking account all week and needed some money to pay bills. He could write checks directly to people we owed. $145 to Kumon for math and reading tutor; $80.00 to pay for sod that neighbors bought and put down, and $420 to pay for first installment to Bishop Leibold School. John threw paper back at me and said that he wasn't paying for anything. He told me I had 10 days to sign dissolution papers or he would sue me and take my pension. I told him that I wanted an attorney to look things over on my behalf and that I had seen someone who referred me to someone else. I told him that I had an appointment a couple of weeks from now. He was extremely angry and started to tell me that he would take half of the money that my parents were putting away for Emily. That account was closed some time ago *because my parents felt he would find a way to take it. A check for $20,000 was sent to my sister for a car loan and the remainder was given back to my dad to secure. John did pick up Emily at 2:15 pm. Did not ask for baby. Paged me to pick her up at 6:45 at J C Penney because he did not want to come to my parents' house where I was having dinner (2 minutes from J C Penney).*

Sunday, July 2

Called John at 9:00 am or so from work and asked him "why the big hurry to sign papers?" and why he was involving or trying to involve and take money from Emily that my parents put away. He said that he was going to report my parents to the IRS if I didn't sign within 10 days. He said he was mad that I wouldn't tell him who had been talking about him and his extra marital activities. He stated that he would no longer continue counseling (concerning our children). He stated that the divorce would be on his terms or he would take everything. John called at dinner time to say that he would go see kids at the house Monday afternoon while I was at work.

Monday, July 3

Babysitter stated that John came to house about 2:30 and spent 2 minutes playing with baby and then went to basement and took a 1 ½ hour nap. When he got up he sent babysitter home and took kids to pool because the house was being shown *at 4:15 pm. I came home from work at 6:00 pm and he left. Opened individual checking account. Transferred $1,200 from joint account (Firstar Bank). National City Bank—joint checking about had >$10,000: I got 2 certified checks—$1,750 to pay balance of loan to parents (overpaid $250 which was returned to me); $1,680 to Bishop Leibold School for 2000-2001 school tuition for Emily Ann.*

Friday, July 7

Post it notes that John left on this date:

1) WHAT TIME CAN I HAVE EMILY TOMORROW

2) HAVE YOU SIGNED DIVORCE PAPERS?

3) DOGS ARE FED

Called regarding taking dogs to vet at 3:30 pm. I asked him if he knew where 2 of my folders were containing legal documents. He said he did not take them. I believed that he did. I told him to be sure to check his account because I had written some checks to pay bills because he was refusing to pay them. He got extremely angry like I had never heard before and said, "Now you've had it, you fucking cunt!" I hung up the phone and called my attorney, his attorney and filed a report with Springboro police. My attorney advised me to get a civil protection order. The post it notes above were on the counter when I got home. I found documents that I was missing. My daughter had taken them into her room.

John was in the house today. Apparently took dogs to vet. Noticed that he had removed our Juno (email) account from the computer.

At the time, I thought it was because things had escalated that I followed the advice of my attorney and immediately filed for a civil protection order (CPO). I would learn later from experts like Laura Richards that women in these situations often know better than anyone how much danger they are in. They know their abuser, and they are the ones most able to accurately assess their situation. I know now that this was when I fully realized how different John had become and just how different my circumstances were. This was just one more example of how important it is for people in these dangerous situations to follow their instincts.

Later that day, the girls and I went for a walk with our neighbor and her children. We must have looked like we didn't have a care in the world—two friends out enjoying a beautiful day with their kids. But really we were heavy with worry. The situation with John continued to escalate, and he felt so unpredictable. When we got home about an hour later, John's car was in my driveway. My blood ran cold. I took the girls to our neighbor's house, told her about the restraining order, and then used her phone to call my house.

When John answered, I asked him if he was on his way out. He angrily replied that he wasn't leaving until I came back to the house and talked to him. I refused, and we were at a stalemate. John claimed he had a legal right to be in the house, but

I knew it wasn't safe for me to meet with him alone, and I had just gotten a protection order.

I hung up the phone and called the Springboro police. They came to talk to me at my neighbor's house first. In the meantime, Emily, five years old at the time, had been playing on the neighbor's patio, unaware of anything that was going on, and decided to walk home. When we realized she had walked home, like she had done a hundred times before, we sent Alex, my neighbor's oldest daughter, to my house to ask Emily to return. John wouldn't let her go.

Two officers arrived and walked with me to my house. I told them the court orders were in my purse, and my purse was in my car, parked in the garage. My car was locked, but it didn't matter, because the window was down and I was able to easily open the door.

My heart sank. My purse was missing.

I went into the house with the officers and found John, sitting on the couch, eating ice cream with Emily. He looked like Father of the Year, snuggled up with a very happy Emily. I could see my daughter taking in the situation, looking at me and the police officers. As much as I tried to shield her from everything that was happening with her father, I couldn't keep everything from her. I scooped her up and let the officers know I'd be back as soon as I had Emily somewhere safe.

I brought Emily back to the neighbor's house and returned home to confront John, again with the support of police officers. I explained to the officers that I had been granted an order of protection and that John couldn't be there. John claimed that he had no idea what I was talking about, and technically he was right because he hadn't been served yet. The officers asked if I had the paperwork proving that the order had been issued, and I said that I did.

"Where's my purse, John?"

I knew he was the only person who could have taken it. I didn't know why he'd taken it, but no one else had access to the garage in the short period of time I had left it in my car.

"It's in my car, where you left it," he replied innocently.

The officer asked him to please get it.

John, both officers, and I walked outside and, sure enough, John pulled my purse and keys from the floor of his car. He handed them to me and I gave the papers to one of the officers, who read them and asked John to turn over the keys to the house and the remote controls to the garage.

Even though I was still reeling a bit from the shock of seeing John's car in my driveway, Emily walking home, and my purse being missing, I still had the presence of mind to tell the officers that, despite what John had told them, I had not been in his car that morning. While it didn't really matter for the enforcement of the restraining order, it mattered to me that they understood that I did not voluntarily get into his vehicle that day or have any other kind of contact with him.

While the officers were there, I mentioned to them that John had two guns. They let John know that his guns would have to be turned over as part of the temporary protection order (TPO). I knew one of the guns was in the safe in the basement of the house, but I didn't know where the other one was. Of course, John lied and said he only had one. I thought it might be in his car, and I requested that they search for it.

They lightly combed through his vehicle, including the trunk, but the car was packed with what appeared to be the result of a shopping spree. There were linens, pots and pans, and all kinds of household items mixed in with John's things. They didn't find the gun, and John and the officers left.

About ten minutes later, one of the officers called to say that John was missing a key to his new house. I tried the three keys he had given to me, and one of them didn't work on any of the doors of my house. I returned it to the officers. As a final security measure, I called our home security company and changed our access code. I was grateful they came out the same day to do so. I can't help but wonder what John's plan would have been if I had not obtained the order of protection that day. He was definitely not going to let me leave with my purse and keys hidden away in his car.

Over the next few weeks, small issues with John bubbled up—like his sudden refusal to sell our house or missed time with the girls. But no issue was as significant as the other gun I knew John had access to.

After John showed up at my house unannounced and fabricated the story about the two of us having spent time together that morning, I became even more diligent in my documentation of our interactions. I contacted one of the officers who had been at the house and expressed my concern about the gun I knew John still had. It was a violation of the CPO, but more importantly, I felt unsafe. I told him that I had two boxes of bullets at the house that proved John also had a 9mm gun. We both knew that alone wasn't enough to do anything, but I had to try, and to his credit, the officer seemed to want to help as well. He said he'd talk to his sergeant, but nothing came of that.

I was also learning the importance of accurate records, because if there was a loophole, John would find it. And a lot of days, it seemed like John was just plain lucky. My best defense was a well-documented approach, so I confirmed with the officer that it had been noted in his report that John had taken my purse and put it in his car.

I didn't know it at the time, but I would be using my expert recording skills like this for years. I struggled to understand how John benefited from constantly picking fights with me over things that I knew didn't actually matter to him, but I also knew that the "why" of John's actions wasn't what was most important at that moment. I was just trying to survive, and to survive, I knew I had to document as much as I could.

Years later I would meet Dr. Christine Cocchiola, who specializes in the traumatic experiences of adult and child victims of coercive control and narcissistic abuse. With her help, I began to understand what John was doing in those early days of our separation. Recently, when Christine and I spoke, something she said really resonated with me.

"It's to inflict pain," she said quite simply. "It's sadistic. Because it hurt you the most. [Narcissists] care more about hurting you than they care about their money." I realized that was true. Even though the way John could cause me pain had changed, he had opportunities to hurt me like no one else, and he loved it. Even if it had meant spending every nickel we had, he would have made our separation as long and difficult as possible.

The day of July 10, 2000, was a bright spot in my terrible separation from John—even if I didn't know it at the time. I met with and officially retained attorney Ellen Rittgers. When I share my story, I talk a lot about the decisions I made, and it's important to me that people know that many of the most critical moments wouldn't have gone as well without her guidance. It's hard enough to navigate the legal system when you aren't familiar with it but doing so while combating a psychopath who's actively seeking revenge is too much for any person to handle alone. John's goal, common among abusers, was to leverage the family court to destroy me financially, professionally, emotionally, and psychologically.

Ellen was one of the people in my corner from the start, and I'll forever recognize that without her, my divorce and custody battle with John would have had a very different outcome. All of my court appearances and filings after this point were done with her support, and as stressful as the experience still was, it was much easier with someone who knew my story helping me along the way.

I made another important decision that same week. After nearly ten years of knowing John, I made the terrifying decision to call his mother.

CHAPTER 9

THE PHONE CALL

This is Tonia. I'm married to your son John.

—TONIA TO DOLORES, JOHN'S MOTHER

When John filed for divorce, I finally accepted that he had given up on our marriage. But I still didn't understand why. John told our counselors that I was acting too much like his mother. He'd routinely say, "I have a mother and don't need another one." He also claimed that he couldn't trust me anymore because I had opened his mail. He couldn't trust me, even though he was the one who had filed for divorce without telling me and while we were still in marriage counseling. I would have fought for our marriage, but it was clear to me that he didn't feel the same way. Something was wrong, and it wasn't a problem I could solve. I could feel it in my gut. We had just had our second child, and yet something was off. For my daughters and for myself, I knew I had to uncover what that something was.

Just a few months earlier, I had been consumed by the normal things a working mother of two young children thinks about. After John chose to leave our young family, I noticed inconsistencies rising to the surface. Something was missing and I needed answers. And if John wasn't going to give them to me, then I knew I needed to find time to figure them out on my own. The John I fell in love with was no longer in front of me and I had no idea why.

Though I had never spoken to her, my gut told me that John's mother would be the best person to give me some answers. I realized, as my marriage crumbled around me, that everything I knew about John's family came directly from John. I hadn't had any reason or opportunity to corroborate anything, and all of my instincts told me that she was who I needed to talk to.

John described his family as terrible, selfish people. He had told me that his father was an embarrassing alcoholic. And I believed him—why would he lie?

With some help I was able to locate a phone number for John's mom. Nervously, I dialed the number, reminding myself that I didn't have anything to lose at this point. When she picked up, I said, "Dolores? Is this Dolores?"

Sounding a little puzzled, she confirmed that she was Dolores. I pushed forward and blurted out, "This is Tonia. I'm married to your son John."

The line was briefly quiet before she said, "Oh, Tonia. I knew you would call me one day."

Like the call I'd experienced so many years earlier when I spoke with a woman who claimed to have slept with my husband the night before, the memories of my call with Dolores are a bit hazy, and I'm so glad I was journaling about what was happening at the time. While I was looking for answers, and to some degree knew that I would learn things I didn't want to know, I wasn't prepared for the long and shocking list of lies I'd uncover that day. Some were small lies with big implications. John had lied about his birthday. I hadn't known his legal name—he seemed to use variations of it over time. These were such strange facts coming from his mother, and yet they all pointed to the same conclusion: I had no idea who the man I had married was.

Dolores also shared stories that were almost too horrible to believe, and yet, after the changes I'd seen in John in the previous months, I was sure they were true. A picture of who John really was began to form.

The first surprising question Dolores asked me on that call was if John was still using drugs. She went on to explain that John had been convicted of a drug charge when he was in college in California. I would later talk to Joe and hear more of the details, but just finding out about the arrest was shocking enough. For any wife, learning that her husband of nearly ten years had kept something of such significance from her would be upsetting. But I'm a nurse anesthetist, and I helped John join my profession. My personal and professional code of ethics—every part of who I am—opposes the abuse of drugs. I have a detailed understanding of how illegal drug use negatively impacts individuals and society. Listening to Dolores, I realized that I had vouched for John and helped him gain entry into the profession I value so deeply.

In his application for school and his license, John would have had to disclose his criminal record—how could he have successfully navigated those requirements without me even knowing it? Once I had time to think about it, I realized that a drug charge isn't what's called an "absolute bar" in most states.

Absolute bars refer to convictions for felonies like aggravated assault or murder. While a drug charge is serious, it wouldn't necessarily prohibit him from obtaining a license.

Dolores shared more about John's upbringing, specifically about his father, Bill. She shared that their household was regularly filled with thinly veiled threats of violence. If people didn't do as Bill wanted, threats were made, and John knew firsthand that many were carried out. I'd discover for myself that John adopted those same techniques as an adult when he threatened me.

She also shared that John's father conspired with him to run multiple cons—from throwing himself in front of a car and then blackmailing the driver to putting glass in his food at Taco Bell and filing a lawsuit. Bill was often the mastermind, but John used much of what he learned in his own life, weaponizing information whenever he had the opportunity.

I could tell that these conversations were difficult for Dolores, and as she continued to share details about John's life, I couldn't blame her for recommending that I reach out to her daughters—the sisters who grew up with John. She felt I'd learn a lot talking to them, so she gave me their contact information, and I reached out.

Talking to Karen and Donna was different from talking to Dolores, though many of the same stories came up. But John's sisters were able to share more about what it felt like to grow up like John did because they had experiences similar to his own. Being Bill's daughter was certainly different from being his son, but their stories still provided great insight into what I was seeing with John as our marriage disintegrated.

Everything I learned from Dolores was shocking. Not only did he have a history of drug use and a serious drug arrest, but

I also learned that he was now mailing potent anesthesia drugs to his brother Dan. I would later hear an even more disturbing story. John's family had always had concerns about their father Bill's passing. I had known that John had visited Bill, and, of course, I had known that he had passed away, but I will always remember the chill that ran down my spine when Donna told the story of John's last visit with his father.

Because of the flexibility of her job, Donna had taken on the care of her father after he had been diagnosed with small-cell lung cancer. She took him to see his doctors and receive chemotherapy. She fixed his meals for the week before returning home. Bill could mostly care for himself and, at the time, just needed that extra support Donna was able to provide; he could still live independently.

That changed on New Year's Eve 1996, when friends of Bill found him collapsing on his bathroom floor. His plan to go out and celebrate the new year changed into a trip to the emergency room. Doctors told Bill that there wasn't anything more they could do for him and that his cancer had progressed to a point where he would now need to transition to hospice care.

Donna called John and said he needed to come out—that he should see Bill while he was still coherent. Because of the separation John had created between me and his family, I didn't know Donna, but I knew she believed it was best for John to see his dad.

I didn't know if John would go. He had always spoken of his family with such derision that I didn't know if he was even interested in pursuing any kind of closure. But I was glad when he agreed to go. I was hopeful it would be an important step toward healing.

But what I didn't know until Karen and Donna shared their experiences with John years later was that the tension in John and Bill's relationship began in high school and increased when John went to college. Like many fathers, Bill continually asked John what he was doing with his life. And like many sons, John resented the fact that Bill didn't support him more financially. They seemed to be at odds constantly, each thinking the other was at fault for the unhealthy dynamic of the relationship.

Donna recalls a watershed moment with John when, after telling his family that he had graduated from both law school and medical school, his father told him to prove it—and if he could prove it, he'd cut him a check right then and there for the tuition John felt Bill owed him. Of course, John had excuses about why he couldn't prove his credentials at that moment, but as the old saying goes, you can't con a con man. Bill and his sisters knew he was lying.

With Bill needing more care as his health continued to decline, Donna stayed and supported him with the help of hospice nurses. Even though he was receiving end-of-life care, he was still alert and communicative during John's visit. They had a routine set up by the time John arrived. The hospice nurse stayed overnight and left in the morning. The day John arrived was no different. The nurse let John and Donna know that they'd be back that evening.

Donna wanted John to have time with his father, and she welcomed the opportunity for a short break to take a shower and rest a bit. Though John and Bill had time alone together, others were in the house, and if needed, she was sure John would ask them for help.

She had barely started her shower when there was a knock on the bathroom door. Irma, a family friend, told her through the door, "Donna, your father has passed."

Shocked, Donna was sure that she hadn't heard her correctly. How could he have died so suddenly and without any indication that his time was imminent?

After quickly getting dressed, she went to see what had happened and found a largely unemotional John, who confirmed that their father had died suddenly. Karen would soon join her siblings and confirm what Donna had suspected. Something was very wrong.

Donna feels confident that she knows—at least in part—what happened to her father that day. Donna had shared with Karen that she had heard an odd exchange—her dad forcefully telling John to "stop giving that shit to me." Not knowing what they were talking about and not wanting to make things worse, she dismissed it at the time.

"Knowing what I know now—how John was carrying around the vials and needles—I think he wanted it all over," Donna would later say, reflecting on her father's final day.

Karen had been flying in that day to see her dad, and when she landed mid-afternoon, her brother Danny picked her up at the airport and told her that their father had passed away. In shock, Karen continued to the house to say her final goodbye, still struggling to understand how her dad could have passed so quickly. At the house, she mourned her father's passing with Donna and Dan. John was already on a plane back home.

"The minute I went into that room, I knew something had happened. Something was wrong. The aura was wrong," Karen, a practicing nurse at the time, would say. "Nurses know. Something's not right. It wasn't peaceful. I just knew it."

Karen spoke with Bill's doctor, who confirmed her suspicion. The only logical explanation for Bill's sudden passing was that he had been given something incorrectly, but they would never know what. I'm still not sure why, but Bill chose John as his healthcare power of attorney. John could and did deny his family's request to explore their father's cause of death. John also had Bill cremated immediately, despite knowing that was not Bill's wish.

Sharing this story leaves me as stunned as I was the first time I heard it, if that even seems possible. I had experienced confusing behavior from John. He was acting like a completely different person, someone I didn't know, not someone I had been in a relationship with for more than a decade. Although I understand and even accept that John was a psychopath, it's still upsetting to think about the pain he caused his family, taking from them the chance to say goodbye to their father.

CHAPTER 10

MY NEW REALITY

That can be gone in a heartbeat.

—JOHN'S RESPONSE WHEN TONIA ASKED ABOUT NATALIE, HIS PREGNANT GIRLFRIEND

On July 17, 2000, I received a call from Dr. Bob, our anesthesiologist friend. Dr. Bob was actually the entire reason John had a job in Michigan. Since John couldn't work as a CRNA in Ohio before taking his boards, we were both so appreciative of Dr. Bob's help when he suggested John work for him in Michigan as a locum tenens. We spoke often, and I had just told him about my conversation with John's mother. John had no idea that our mutual friend and I had been talking, and he certainly didn't know we had formed a kind of secret alliance. So when he called to say that John had asked him to go to dinner, we both wondered if something was up.

I eagerly waited to hear how their dinner went. When he called to report what he and John had talked about, he said he had told John that I had talked to his mother and that the blood drained from John's face. Apparently, he immediately picked up the phone to call his mother, but she didn't answer.

Returning to the moment, John asked Bob what his mother had told me, and Bob pretended not to know, even though I had shared the details of what I had learned with him. He just told John his impression was that "it was some serious shit."

Within a few minutes, John paged me and asked if I had called his mother. I told him yes, and he quickly asked just what she had told me.

"Why don't you just start by telling me the truth?" I asked him.

He demanded again that I tell him what she said, and I replied with the same question. Accepting that neither of us was going to budge, he said that I had done exactly what he had told me never to do. He switched tactics and told me that now, because of what I had done, he was going to have to shoot himself.

"Tonia, I'm going to do it. Do you want them to find my body in this hotel?"

I told him that nothing was so bad that he had to kill himself, but he couldn't seem to calm down. He then proceeded to tell me a new story—that he had worked for the DEA for five years, including two years in South America. He told me he had "put a hundred guys in prison" and that they would want him dead. He said he had kept that secret to protect me.

I couldn't quite figure out where this was coming from, but the floodgates had opened. In a rushed and rambling tirade, he admitted to having three affairs, that he had a girlfriend in Michigan, that he had been sending his brother Dan the drug Versed in the mail. I don't know what he thought his mother told me or why he was telling me all of this now, but oddly enough, he stuck to one lie.

He denied using drugs himself.

I told him that I had been watching the drug box in his office closet and had noticed that it went missing the day after I asked him about the syringe in his suitcase. I told him that I had counted eight vials of fentanyl at one time and the last time I had access to the box there were only four. Where had those drugs gone? He said he put the drug box in the sump pump in the basement, but he never addressed the missing vials. I later checked the sump pump and I didn't see the box. I wasn't surprised. I didn't really expect John to tell me where he hid the drugs.

And I knew John was hiding other things from me. I had heard from my friend Dr. Bob that John had big things happening in his life. The doctor he was dating in Michigan was pregnant and John was going to ask her to marry him. Dr. Bob and I agreed that John was definitely proposing out of desperation because his new, successful girlfriend was his safety net, but it still felt like salt in my wound. Even though John had shown his true colors and I didn't want us to get back together, I had always wanted a third child. It felt like now my husband was having that child with another woman.

By this point, I had figured out—subconsciously and then intentionally—to practice the technique known today as "gray rocking" when I was talking to John. Narcissists thrive on the reactions they can get out of their victims, and gray rocking means responding unemotionally to an abuser's comments, denying them the reactions they are seeking. I didn't really know yet that John was a narcissist or psychopath, though people had certainly suggested it. I hadn't fully developed techniques for dealing with him, but I had learned that refusing to react to his heightened emotional states upset him. And when he was upset, I had an advantage.

So, seeing that the shocking news he was revealing had no effect on me, he pivoted again and asked if there was a chance that we could reconcile. I wasn't considering it, of course, but my immediate response was, "What about your pregnant girlfriend?"

"That can be gone in a heartbeat," was his flat, immediate reply.

That. He had just referred to his girlfriend and the mother of his child as *that*—a problem that could simply be removed. Did he mean he would break up with her, or kill her? I wondered how often Emily, Abby, and I were referred to in the same way.

The roller coaster continued when he realized I wasn't interested in reconciling. He brought up the terms of our divorce and threatened to keep fighting them; he then apologized, and then threatened to take half my pension. After that, he seemed to return to trying to hurt my feelings again by saying he knew our marriage had been over for five years. I could barely keep up with him—he was all over the map.

When I finally got a word in—after he said he had felt our relationship had been over for years—I asked him why he had agreed to have another baby. Why, if he was so sure we weren't going to make it, had he been interested in growing our family?

In a defeated voice, he muttered, "I thought it would help."

Help what, exactly? At the time, his response didn't make any sense to me. Now I believe that John thought a second baby would distract me, making it easier for him to continue his escapades outside of our marriage. I'm sure that's not what he wanted me to think at that moment, but maybe it was an accidental bit of honesty.

We had both run out of energy at this point, and John shifted the conversation to what he wanted. He said that he wouldn't have me served with divorce papers if I amended the CPO to allow him visitation. I told him that I wanted him to take a drug test first, and he agreed. He said that I would have to take one too, which of course I agreed to. He said, "Just tell me the place and time," which, in retrospect, makes sense. He was taking fentanyl and Versed, and both are out of your system quickly. Drug tests weren't a problem for him, because all he needed was a little warning and he could pass them without any issue.

On July 18, just a day after John's meltdown, my parents went with me to meet Ellen, my attorney, for a court hearing. I told Ellen that I wasn't expecting John to show up because Dr. Bob was keeping me informed of John's every move. I understood that, like Dr. Bob, Ellen was my ally, and I needed to keep her informed, so I made sure she was aware of everything that had happened.

As predicted, John was not present in court, and his attorney scrambled a bit before asking for a continuance. We met before the magistrate and set a new court date for August 17, 2000, with the CPO in effect. The attorneys still wanted to meet prior to the next court date to see if we could come to an agreement on a few matters. I was officially served with divorce papers.

That afternoon, John called me to find out what had happened in court. I told him he should call his attorney. He said he was going to have his attorney stop the divorce but was unable to get ahold of him prior to the hearing, and that is why I was served with papers. But what he was saying just didn't ring true.

Even though I'd never know exactly what John was thinking, I could see that his plan was backfiring. He wasn't in control like he thought he would be.

The next week, John's mom called me, concerned because John had tried to call her six times that day. She also said that John had written her a letter. She wanted to know what was going on. I told her that John knew that we had spoken, and then I held my breath waiting for her response. On one hand, she knew he'd find out we had talked. But on the other hand, we both knew what this meant for her. Dolores and I talked for nearly forty-five minutes, and I was so relieved to hear how understanding she was. I suppose it makes sense—she had more experience than anyone living with the fear of John's inevitable retaliation. We talked about getting together soon so she could spend time with the girls, something John had worked so hard to prevent.

I was also having conversations with Karen about her kids, whom she had shared pictures of, but also about John and any new information she may have learned. She shared that, before I knew him, John had successfully implemented multiple cons. He had staged an accident with a friend for the insurance money, allowing himself to actually be hit by a car, though he wasn't too seriously injured. He also intentionally slammed on his brakes so that he would be rear-ended and collected $25,000 from his insurance company. Karen reiterated the story of how John put glass in his food at a Taco Bell and successfully sued the company, even though he didn't actually eat any glass or have proof that he had been harmed. Each story she shared seemed more unbelievable than the last, and yet, I was getting to the point where I didn't think anything could surprise me anymore.

At this point in our separation, I was also learning a lot about psychology and what was really happening with John. In talking to my therapist, I had to agree with her that John claiming to be suicidal, pleading with me to reconcile, and picking fights over furniture were all behaviors that indicated he was an addict and that he was getting desperate. My therapist noted specifically that his threat of suicide was a manipulation technique. For the first time, in a serious context, she also talked to me about the very real possibility that he had a personality disorder. She couldn't diagnose him, of course, and I was only just beginning to understand how important it was to my survival to understand what truly was wrong with John. I filed the idea away in my mind, and I'd build on it later.

More pressing was the question of how to talk to Emily about John and his alarming behavior. At five years old, she was aware of some of what was happening—it just wasn't possible to hide everything from her, so what was I supposed to tell her? My choices may have screwed my life up, but I was going to make every effort known to man to keep my kids' lives from being screwed up too. I asked my counselor for a recommendation for Emily, and I got her into counseling.

A year earlier, I hadn't been in contact with anyone in John's family, but now I was having frequent conversations with his mom and sister. The girls and I were continuing our plans to see John's mom and sister Karen in September of 2000. Though my conversations with John's family were often light and focused on our upcoming trip, we would inevitably talk about more things John had been doing that I hadn't known about. One of these instances was related to John's brother Dan. Karen made a comment that, when John had been in San Francisco, he had connected with Dan and given him cocaine. Because of this connection, and what we all knew of Dan's addiction, we decided that we had to be careful about what we shared with Dan, especially in any conversations about John. But in August, I did connect with Cathy, Dan's wife, who was concerned about her husband's relationship with John.

While I was hearing stories from John's family, John was hearing that we had all been talking and nothing infuriated him more. The day after I talked to Cathy, John paged me, and I responded quickly; there was no point avoiding him. When he answered, he was so worked up, he was out of breath.

He told me that he knew I had been talking to his family and now he was going to bring *my* family into this. He said he'd tell them he was "fucking me up the ass in the basement." He listed people closest to me: my parents, Uncle Jim, Aunt Mae, and Uncle Andy.

Unhinged, he couldn't seem to focus on any one line of threats. After describing how he planned to humiliate me in front of my family, he switched back to legal threats, saying that I was going to perjure myself on the stand, because I knew that he was born in 1959 since I had seen his driver's license the night we met. "How are you planning to get out of that?" he asked menacingly.

The next topic he tackled was visitation, claiming that soon he'd have the girls three days every week. This was so far from possible, I couldn't help myself—I pointed out that, with his drug use, he wouldn't get custody and, honestly, he'd be lucky if he kept his CRNA license.

Frustrated that I wasn't threatened by anything he was saying, he went back to the only thing he knew would bother me. He told me the phone calls to my family would start that night.

I did what I could to prepare everyone. I talked to my dad and told him that if John called, he should just hang up on him. But John didn't catch my parents at home. He left vulgar messages on their answering machine that afternoon. I saved and eventually transcribed them.

> *Hey John and Mary, this is John, and I guess Tonia has been talking to my family members and causing a bit of a problem and I think I should just explain to you—as much as we all have dark sides, so does Tonia and your daughter really had a penchant for anal sex so you know I thought I'd just let you know about that. She's not as clean and as pure as you think she is, so I hope you both have a good day.*

John ended the call, then immediately called back and left a second message.

> *Hey Mary and John, just one other thing. I just wanted to let you know that I took your daughter home on the first night. Didn't even know her name. Just took her home and had our way with each other. See, your daughter isn't as clean and as pure as you think she is. There's a lot about her that we're all going to find out. It ain't gonna be pretty and I just wanted you guys to know that it's Tonia's fault for picking up the phone and making some phone calls to some family members of mine. I think I'll call Uncle Andy and Aunt Mae next. Let them know what's in on this. Bye.*

Accepting that harassing phone calls to my friends and family was my new reality, my dad and I went to RadioShack and bought a tape recorder to record my parents' answering machine.

Later that week, I got home from work around seven thirty and had an unexpected message on my answering machine.

> *Yes, my name is Charlie. I'm calling from Brinks Home Security in regards to a request that was put in to cancel the service. I need to speak with you before I can cancel the service, so if you could just give me a call back...*

I hadn't requested that my security system be canceled, of course—John had. Maybe he didn't realize what the verification process would be or maybe he thought he was still on the account. I wondered if he wanted to turn off the security system so that he could access the house—maybe to retrieve drugs he'd hidden, or even to kill me. Maybe he was just finding new and creative ways to ensure I couldn't have a moment of peace.

I called the Springboro Police Department and one of the officers who had been at our house when John was given the restraining order came out. He listened to the message and created the report I would need for court. It was a violation of the CPO, so it was important that everything be done by the book.

Out of an abundance of caution, Emily stayed at a friend's house and Abby and I stayed with my parents that night. In the morning, we went to the police station to pick up the reports I'd need for court. The officer we met with advised me to change the locks.

In the afternoon, I went to the CPO hearing with my parents. We were early, but John was already there, meeting with his attorney. We were waiting in separate areas, but at one point

I had to walk past him to go to the water fountain. I did not make eye contact. On the way back, John started to stomp his foot on the tile to simulate that he was chasing me. It sent chills up my spine. I could feel how much he was enjoying this.

The attorneys met with the magistrate for more than forty-five minutes. Ellen came out to notify me that John and I were both ordered to give hair samples for drug testing and that John was going to get visitation starting Sunday. I was horrified that John would have a visitation before we received the results of the drug test. We negotiated drop-off and pick-up details, and then John became angry. In that moment, I think he didn't fully understand what drugs would be tested for in the hair sample, but he did know he didn't have any way to avoid the test. He said he'd forfeit visitation until our divorce hearing on August 30. I still don't know why he did this, but I'm confident there was a reason. Regardless, my relief was palpable.

I immediately went for my drug test, feeling confident that this step would be exactly what my case needed. When they were filling out paperwork, I noticed that they didn't test for benzodiazepines. Disappointed, I asked for more information and one of the techs called the lab for me. She confirmed they wouldn't test for benzos like Versed or synthetic opiates like fentanyl—there would be no indication of the drugs John was taking because they weren't yet routinely abused substances.

I called Ellen immediately to explain what was happening. She said it was good that we knew, but there wasn't anything we could do about it. I was disappointed, now understanding that John likely wouldn't fail the drug test and bring our court battle to a close. Instead, our deposition and court appearances continued on, and I was forced to continue sending my girls for visitations.

It was becoming clear to me that one part of John's strategy would be intimidation. I remember one instance when John's attorney started questioning me, and John began posturing and smirking at me in an attempt to throw me off balance. Thank goodness Ellen recognized his tactics and didn't let that happen for long. She had me moved so John couldn't continue his attempts to intimidate me.

John had fed his attorney stories—some true, some false, and some a combination of fact and fiction—designed to discredit me as a medical professional and, ultimately, as a person. He even accused me of things that confirmed his crimes, like claiming that I had always known his real date of birth and had gone along with him sharing false information.

One of the most upsetting stories that his attorney brought up was John's best attempt to paint me as someone who abused my position as a nurse anesthetist like he had. Early in our marriage, I brought ketamine and Norcuron home from the hospital where I was working, so that we could put our beloved dog Nikki to sleep in the comfort of her own home. At the time, ketamine wasn't a controlled substance, and the vial I took was partially empty and would have been discarded in the trash at the end of the day.

John knew that I would tell the truth, and he would use this testimony given under oath to show that it was I who had a history of removing a drug from the hospital. John testified that he held the dog under my "direction" while I gave the injections. Actually, John had volunteered to put our dog to sleep because my family was having a difficult time making the decision. Nikki was terrified of the vet's office, and we didn't want his last moments to be filled with fear, so this seemed like the best option. Bawling my eyes out, I held Nikki while John gave a shot of ketamine. Once the dog stopped moving, I waited a minute or two and then pinched him. He didn't flinch, so I told John he was asleep, and John gave a second injection of Norcuron to paralyze him. I confirmed that his heart had stopped, and John buried him in the backyard where my dad had already dug a hole.

Thirty years ago, it wasn't unheard-of for a surgeon or anesthesia provider to take home an unused non-controlled substance to euthanize a pet. Thinking about that choice now, I realize I technically shouldn't have taken the leftover medication home for personal use, but at the time it didn't seem like a big deal. I didn't even think twice about it. Together, we administered the drug so that our dog could pass peacefully. In that moment, was John already thinking about how it could be used against me if needed? John was so skilled at gathering evidence against people, I have to wonder.

As I listened to John's attorney ask about that day—as he emphasized that, under my direction, John used the drugs that I had taken from the hospital—I could see that this was all he could come up with to hold against me. A questionable but not unheard-of practice from years ago, retold to make John look as innocent as possible, was as close as he'd be able to get to destroying my reputation and trying to pin the drugs found in our home on me. Would it work? Could he make people believe that I couldn't be trusted because I was someone who had removed substances from the hospital?

On Monday, September 4, 2000, Emily called me from John's house just to talk. I was glad to hear her voice. She said she was having a good time. In the adorable way that children do, she rambled on, jumping from one unrelated topic to another. She was excited that her daddy was going to move to a farm and buy her a horse and that he knew someone who would teach her how to ride a horse. He promised to buy her a trampoline. She said he didn't have any furniture because he was only going to live there for a few weeks. This is where the post-separation lies and broken promises started for my daughters. It would take a little time, but they would figure it all out. I never had to utter a word.

Despite being so young, she was thinking about me that day. She wanted to know what I did last night and what I was going to do that day. She was like a ray of sunshine in all of the darkness that John brought with him.

I had an uneventful rest of the day and went to bed. I woke from a deep sleep a little before midnight when my phone rang. John's sister Karen was calling to tell me that their brother Dan had overdosed. His wife had found him unresponsive on their couch and paramedics were unable to revive him.

Though time had passed since John's dad had died, the family was still grieving that loss. Dan's death on top of that was almost too much to bear. Karen was nearly hysterical when she called me and asked me to tell John, in no uncertain terms, that he was not welcome at the funeral.

I paged John "911" as soon as I got off the phone with Karen. He called back immediately, and I let him know that Dan had overdosed.

"Thanks for the call," he said and hung up.

CHAPTER 11

LIVING SEPARATE LIVES

[Narcissists] do not know how to authentically love. They do not. And therefore they never authentically love the children. They never do.

—DR. CHRISTINE COCCHIOLA

By September of 2000, just a few months after I found out John had filed for divorce without telling me, I was functioning well in my strange new reality. I had sent flowers to Dolores and Dan's wife, Cathy, to let them know I was thinking of them in the wake of Dan's overdose. I called Ellen to let her know that John hadn't paid his child support or the back pay arrears required. What a different life I was living today compared to a year ago. And these extra tasks weren't the worst of it. John continued to demonstrate that he was someone I no longer knew. I suppose he was someone I had never known.

I was initially so confident that John would fail his drug screening. Learning that he had passed was difficult for me to accept. It was so frustrating to continually see him luck out. Of course, John knew how frustrated this was making me, knowing how horrible he was without being able to prove it. When he eventually sent his child support payment for the week, he left a notation in the comment line:

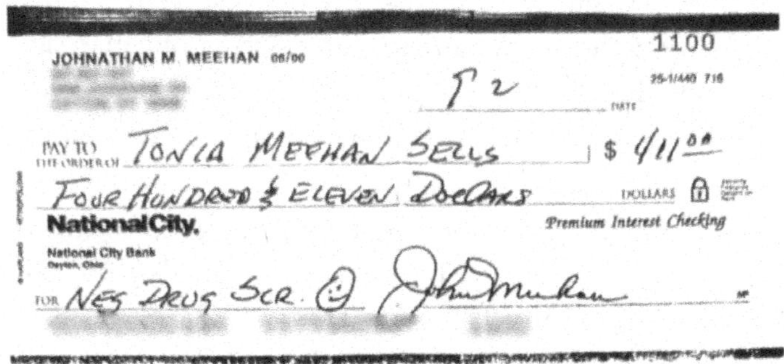

JOHNATHAN M. MEEHAN 08/00

1100

25-1/440 716

7 2 DATE

PAY TO THE ORDER OF TONIA MEEHAN SELLS $ 411.00

FOUR HUNDRED & ELEVEN DOLLARS DOLLARS

NationalCity.

Premium Interest Checking

National City Bank
Dayton, Ohio

FOR NEG DRUG SCR. ☺

I wanted to scream, "Isn't his writing 'Neg Drug Screen :)' flaunting the fact that he beat the system proof that he shouldn't be allowed to work in the medical field? How is this not evidence that his time alone with our children is a danger to them?" But I had learned by now that it wasn't enough, so I made a copy of the check and added it to my ever-growing pile of evidence against him.

About a week after Dan died, I called Karen to see how everyone was doing. She shared that John had called Dan's house, despite being asked not to engage with the family, to say that he "heard through the grapevine" that his brother had died. I wasn't surprised that he had ignored their wishes, but I was a little surprised to learn the details of the stories John told her.

Presumably to discourage his family from speaking with me, John told Karen that I was telling people that Dan committed suicide because of him. Of course I hadn't, but I'm sure

John realized his family would make the connection between his drug abuse and Dan's overdose. Did John know that his family would blame him for Dan's death? Was he laying the groundwork to garner sympathy and avoid responsibility for this tragedy within his family even before anyone directly accused him?

He also told Karen what he had told the women he was dating—that I was the one having an affair during our marriage. And for something new, he added that my parents had somehow laundered $250,000. I didn't know where he was getting these ideas. What he was saying was so random, it was almost as if he was watching the gangster movies he loved so much, extracting storylines, and trying to convince people they were true in some part of his life. It would have been laughable if John weren't so terrifying.

Karen shared all of this with me and seemed unmoved by John's claims. It was clear that John knew he hadn't persuaded his family, because after their call, John had started emailing Karen threatening messages. It seemed she was receiving the same hot-and-cold treatment so many people in John's life had experienced. John was becoming frustrated with her lack of response to his attempts to gain sympathy and instill fear, but like me, Karen had seen who John really was and couldn't be easily manipulated.

As our separation dragged on, we had yet another court appearance, where John requested a reduction in child support because he was going to have surgery the following week. His request was denied. He requested a change in his visitation schedule so that he would have the girls on my days off. That request was different because the visitation schedule had a temporary status, so changes had to be discussed by everyone involved instead of being determined by a ruling. We declined John's request for the change in schedule.

His last request was to take the girls with him to Disney World. He was going to Florida for a meeting and wanted to bring the girls to the theme park. I was so confused and I didn't know why the magistrate wasn't catching the faulty logic in his requests. How was he going to go to a meeting and take care of two young children? Why did he have money for a vacation but no money for child support? How was he going to tote the girls around Disney World after he had just had back surgery? So much didn't make sense, but we talked about one item at a time, and in evaluating each one, it was as if the other items weren't even being considered. Was I the only one who could see the big picture that made it so obvious who John really was?

No decisions were made that day about the trip. John had already told Emily that he was taking her to Disney World, and he would be allowed to in just a few months. That day in September, though, it wasn't top-of-mind. I left the courthouse and continued on with my investigation.

My close friends, John and Lois Schikner, were amazingly supportive. John Schikner came to nearly every court appearance with me, and he and Lois often invited me and the girls to their house to have dinner and just relax. They were also there for me when I had difficult tasks to take on. It was John Schikner's idea to download the hard drive of our home computer so that we could learn more about what John had really been up to.

I wouldn't have even thought to examine the contents of our computer, but Mr. Schikner not only suggested it—he connected me with someone to get the task done. The content was overwhelming because it went back years, outlining John's cheating and saying terrible things about me, but also because it was just a lot of information to sort through. Those dear friends helped with all of that, and I don't think I could have pulled it all together without them.

I had asked my attorney about retrieving material from our hard drive to use in court. I assumed it would be fair game because it was our shared computer, but there was no precedent. We decided to err on the side of caution and not use it. But Ellen advised that I call the prosecutor and give him all of the other evidence that I had that John was stealing drugs, possibly using them and mailing them to Dan in California. The prosecutor's office referred me to Commander John Burke of Warren County's Drug Task Force (WCDTF). This was an indirect route to helping build my case against John, but if it worked as I was hoping, it would be effective in proving that he should not be given custody of the girls.

In my first call with Burke, we spoke for about twenty minutes. I asked him if retrieving deleted information from our hard drive would be illegal. He said, "Absolutely not."

That was all I needed to hear. Without telling them that I had already opened it, I convinced Burke and Detective Tim Parker that I was certain it would contain incriminating evidence against John, and they agreed to take a look. Ultimately, their forensic computer expert could tell the hard drive had been accessed, so none of the information could be submitted as evidence. The problem was that they couldn't see what I had accessed or if I had changed anything. They could only see that I *could have* tampered with it and added incriminating evidence. Anyone who knew me would know I would have no clue as to how to tamper with evidence on a computer, but the law is the law. And besides, the information was still valuable in helping us pull together details that would help my case.

In our short conversation, Burke shared an already well-formulated plan. He told me that Elaine Jones from the pharmacy board and another detective would be contacting me early the following week.

By the end of September, I was having detailed conversations with Detective Parker about John's drug use and diversion and my concerns for the girls' safety. One afternoon, he came by the house unannounced as John was leaving. He and John made eye contact, but John wouldn't have realized he was a police officer because Parker was in an unmarked car. To be safe, Tim kept driving and then called me at home to confirm that John had left and that I was free to meet.

I took the kids to my neighbor's house and, when Detective Parker arrived, we talked for almost an hour about the fraud John had committed, the syringes I had found in the house, everything his family had told me, and the death of his brother. As Tim organized everything we discussed, he mentioned that John didn't have an Ohio driver's license, so I gave him a copy of his Tennessee license.

Sitting in my kitchen that day, feeling more confident than I ever thought I would be assisting in a criminal investigation, I asked Detective Parker if he could subpoena John's computer so that we could look for evidence that he was sending Dan drugs. I knew there was proof he was talking to Dan about mailing diverted drugs on that computer—and there was. But I never anticipated everything else I would find.

On that fall afternoon, though, Tim was still focused on gathering every type of evidence possible. He asked me to show him the stolen drug needles and syringes I had found and exactly where they had been hidden. I showed him John's office and the closet where I had found the red cedar box with fentanyl and Versed in it. I told him that I had planned to take pictures of the box and log its contents, but the box disappeared from the house after I asked John about the syringe. I also told him that when I confronted John on the phone about the box and asked him where it went, he told me it was in the sump pump. I told him that I had looked in there and it wasn't there. Parker immediately asked to see it so he could have a look for himself. I walked him over and lifted the lid, and we both stared into the darkness. He asked me to get a flashlight, and then, with the light, because he was standing on a different side of the sump pump, he spotted the box tucked into the wall. It felt like I had won the lottery but instantly lost all the money. Even though I wanted to find the drug box, it was just another reminder of the disturbing things John had done.

The box still contained a few vials of non-controlled substances, a key fob, and antibiotic ointment. There was also a bottle of red nail polish. The nail polish seemed odd to me, but I realized that the vials of fentanyl had a red ring around them. Was he opening the vials and then trying to make them look like they had been sealed by using red nail polish to replace the red ring?

In October of 2000, John had back surgery, and even though we were divorcing and he was starting a new family, I was on the hook for dealing with all of the drama that came with it. Two days before his surgery, John called and left me a message saying that I had to make sure his surgery was covered by insurance. He demanded that I fax a copy of our insurance card to his attorney and that, if I didn't, I was going to have to pay for his surgery. It wasn't even worth an argument. I sent his insurance information and, as was my new routine, I recorded his hostile message.

The day of John's surgery, I received a message from a hospital employee who had been with John in the operating room. They told me that John had premedicated himself by giving a nurse an order to give him 25 mg of Demerol. The nurse reported that John told her that his anesthetist said he could have it.

She went on to say that John took a lot of meds during surgery and insisted on having a Demerol PCA (patient-controlled analgesia) pump. That would allow John to decide when he would receive additional medicine. Even with that, he had breakthrough pain. She finally got to the heart of why she had called. She had serious concerns for John and for the people around him.

She expressed her belief that John was an addict, and that what she witnessed that day just couldn't be ignored. She also shared that John's anesthetist had told people in the room that John had been bringing a gun to work. This aligned with and heightened concerns they already had after observing how paranoid he had been acting lately.

I continued to hear from mutual friends that John was struggling. On October 10, he didn't show up for work, but by the 11th he was working in Michigan. By the 12th and 13th, he was working his regular shifts again, so he must have given them an acceptable reason for his absence. But then, on the 14th, he showed up as a patient in the emergency room, reporting that he had an infection.

A day later, John was back in the hospital complaining of a spinal headache—a headache that is worse when sitting or standing, forcing sufferers to lie down just to manage the pain.

A mutual friend visited him and reported that he was falling asleep mid-sentence and waking up a few minutes later. John was eventually released after a few days in the hospital, though I never heard his official diagnosis.

Despite living in different states, I would still get calls for and about John. We were still legally married and working in the same field, so we had a lot of connections. In mid-October, John's supervisor at Good Samaritan Hospital reached out, looking for John because he had missed a scheduled shift. Of course, I had no idea where John was. I had long since lost track of his daily schedule, but I did tell his supervisor that he needed to open his eyes—I said John working at their hospital was a very big problem, but that was all I could tell him.

His supervisor said that he had been hearing similar rumors. Employers can't act on rumors, but I was glad to hear that he was at least aware of the potential risks John posed working in the hospital.

Over the next few months, I heard more and more alarming stories about John, particularly about his health. It seemed as if his back issues and drug use were colliding to make him miserable at best, and, on some days, unable to function.

On October 18, he returned to the emergency room, still complaining of a spinal headache, looking for meds for his back spasms. The professionals treating him would give me updates, sharing that he was nervous and jittery and hadn't bathed. The staff at his surgeon's office was aware of the concerns people had about his drug use and refused his request for more prescription pain medicine. Apparently John left and then called five minutes later, hoping to connect with a different nurse, but they had all been warned. John's attempts to secure more drugs through the doctor's office had failed that day, but I knew he was resourceful. I suspected he'd find another way.

Just a few days later, John was back to work and had time scheduled with the girls. Knowing what I did about his health, I was concerned that he may not be able to take care of them, but he hadn't said anything about it. I paged John to confirm he was still planning to see the girls, and he said, "Yes, anything else?"

I asked him if he was off all the prescriptions he had been taking, and he repeated, "Anything else?" I had no choice but to let him know that I was aware of the health issues he was having. I pointed out that if he had a spinal headache, he should not be lifting the baby. He continued with the same reply: "Anything else?"

There was nothing more I could say. I told him that he owed the babysitter fifty-five dollars, and we hung up.

At the end of October, Karen called to let me know that Dan's toxicology report had finally come in. She wanted to know what nordiazepam was. They had found it in Dan's system, along with cocaine, Valium, and Vicodin, but they didn't know what it was. I shared that nordiazepam is an active metabolite of Valium. People take it to treat insomnia, anxiety, muscle spasms, and seizures, but it's only for short-term use because it is so potentially addictive. Learning what substances were in Dan's system helped answer some questions, but it wasn't anything I could use in court against John. It did, however, deepen my belief that John directly contributed to Dan's addiction and death.

In November, still not a year had passed since we separated, and John was granted permission by the courts to take Emily to Disney World for four days. He only asked to take Emily, the older and easier-to-care-for child, on this special trip. I was upset that Emily would be taken out of state and so far from me and equally upset that John was treating Abby so carelessly. Even though she was still a baby, I struggled to understand how he could separate the girls and treat them so differently. I was ordered to give him some clothes and toys, so I agreed to also give him some other items from the house. That was a particularly hard day.

A few weeks earlier, our friend and my new confidant, Dr. Bob, had shared that John bragged to him about buying a $10,000 engagement ring for his girlfriend, who agreed to marry him a few days later. The idea of John and his pregnant fiancée taking Emily on a vacation made me sick to my stomach. I was glad Emily wouldn't be alone with John and I knew she would be safer with another adult there to care for her, but thinking of them acting like a family on a vacation was overwhelming.

I made sure to verify Emily's flight and hotel, so I felt more confident that the travel plans were legitimate. The trip to Disney was ultimately uneventful. Emily called me once from the hotel to say that she was having fun. I did the best I could not to worry, but it felt like she was gone for an eternity. Finally, on November 30, 2000, I was able to write in my journal, "Emily home and back to me at 4:00 p.m."

In December, a friend of mine asked me if I'd speak to John's coworker and fellow CRNA Randy Klotz. Randy had asked to speak with me; I didn't really know what about, but I could have guessed—and I would have been right. I agreed to the call.

Randy shared that he had seen John remove Demerol from a box before returning it to the pharmacy. It had been left in the room by someone else, so John returned it, without the Demerol, and proceeded to get a new box to use for the surgery.

After witnessing this firsthand, he began remembering other details—pieces of information that alone weren't too alarming but together painted a concerning picture. He remembered that, when they were building their narcotic boxes, John was the one who insisted that Demerol be included. The last straw for Randy was when an RN came to him reporting that she had seen John sign out four amps of Demerol and watched him put two of them in his briefcase. Randy knew conclusively that his suspicions were now a reality and that action had to be taken to stop John.

Randy presented his concerns to the physician anesthesiologist and head of the department, but he felt as though they were not taken seriously afterward. It wasn't until he and another RN went to the pharmacy to report their concerns that any action was taken. As a result of the multiple reports, there would be a meeting the following week with hospital officials and John. Until then, he wasn't allowed to work in the hospital. After a more thorough review of John's charts, the anesthesiologist eventually agreed that there definitely seemed to be a problem.

John, Detective Parker, pharmacy representatives, and the anesthesiologist, who was the chief of the anesthesia department and had since concurred that there was an issue with John's charting of narcotics, met at the hospital. John immediately dismissed the police from the meeting to avoid incriminating himself. I guess his law school days had taught him he could ask them to leave. He then asked the anesthesiologist to step out into the hall to speak privately, leaving Elaine Jones from the pharmacy board and the hospital pharmacist.

When they returned, the anesthesiologist completely rescinded all of his concerns and said that John was a good anesthetist. I spoke with Parker right after the meeting and he shared that everyone in attendance was not only shocked but felt betrayed by this drastic turn of events.

I've always assumed John blackmailed the anesthesiologist. We will never know what he had on him, but it's the only thing that makes sense for how that bizarre meeting concluded. We'd all soon learn that John's MO was to have something incriminating on everyone he knew and use it as a weapon when he needed it to save his own ass.

Outside the hospital, John had other issues piling up, though I'm not sure if he knew it. A DEA agent had been assigned to his case, but he hadn't been arrested. Toward the end of his next visitation, he asked to bring the girls back to me a day early, which I gladly agreed to. Although the meeting at the hospital went sideways, on December 11, John was officially suspended from Good Samaritan Hospital. He skipped his visitation with the girls, which was again a relief to me. I knew that some evidence—even if it wasn't everything we needed—was coming together in various cases against him, so every day it became less safe for the girls to be with him, even if the courts didn't agree.

Temporary orders stated John would have the girls for Christmas Eve and half of Christmas Day, two weeks later. He dropped them off at my parents' house in the afternoon on Christmas Day and didn't even pull into the driveway. He brought Abby to the door without a hat or coat—still a baby, she was exposed to the cold winter weather, and John was unfazed. He saw them again on New Year's Eve and shared that he'd need to change his visitation arrangements again because he was working a new job in Michigan.

When I reached out to John about his need to change his visitation arrangements, a woman answered the phone. I asked for John, and she told me I had the wrong number. I called again and when she answered, I called her by her name—I just knew I had the right number and that I was talking to John's new fiancée.

"Yes," she replied.

"Is John there?" I asked.

She hesitated and said no, he wasn't there.

I asked where I could reach him, and she replied with a question of her own:

"Who is calling?"

I said, "Tonia," and she immediately gave me his new pager number. When he returned my page, I told him I wouldn't change the visitation schedule we agreed on, which obviously upset him. We went back and forth for about fifteen minutes about his current situation. He'd complain that I was asking for too much from him and that he had his own rent to pay. Then he'd change gears and threaten to get my license restricted or revoked. It was incredible to think that when 1999 became 2000, John and I were in counseling, managing what I thought were pretty normal challenges associated with having busy schedules and a new baby. When 2000 became 2001, we were divorcing, and he was both engaged to another woman and being investigated by the DEA.

CHAPTER 12

JOHN, YOU WROTE YOUR OWN STORY

Reporting me to the police and DEA is going to make me lose my job, Tonia.

—JOHN MEEHAN, JANUARY 2001

In January of 2001, I had a conversation with John's fiancée for the first time. Aside from our quick exchange when she gave me John's pager number, we hadn't yet crossed paths. But our mutual friend, Dr. Bob, paged me 911, and when we connected, he asked me if I'd speak with her. I agreed and learned later that she had come to our friend that day in tears with questions about John, and Bob did not hold back.

She apologized to me and said that John had told her that we were separated before they had even met. John had claimed that Abby wasn't his and that our marriage had been over for a long time. She had felt sorry for him. We talked about the fact that he was lying about his age, that he had an arrest record, that I felt he had drug problems. I even told her about his brother's death, and that his family and I believed he had played a role in his overdose.

I can't imagine what hearing this information—some of it new, some of it a confirmation of what she had suspected—must have felt like. I had experienced similar revelations, arguably more shocking because I had known John for so much longer, but she was hearing so much, so fast. All the women John was involved with had uniquely terrifying experiences. And, like mine, hers was compounded by the baby they were having together—and by what I said to her next.

I told her that he had been fired from Good Samaritan for bringing a loaded gun to work and that a nurse had seen him putting Demerol in his briefcase. She must have known that he had left his other job, but I'm sure that's not the story he told her, because she would have been obligated to report what she knew to their shared employer, for the safety of their patients and staff.

On that call, she told me she was going to kick him out of their house. I could tell that her head was spinning, and I certainly didn't blame her. I provided what words of support I could, but I knew there was nothing I could say that would help. She was at the beginning of a journey similar to mine, and I knew just how scary that stage was.

What I didn't see coming was a phone call later that evening from Dr. Bob telling me in no uncertain terms that I needed to get out of town. We both knew that John would likely have learned of my talking to his fiancée and he would be furious that I had intervened.

In survival mode, I called Detective Parker and the Miami Township police to let them know what was happening. Then I packed up the girls and we stayed at my parents' house. Thinking John may check there, we hid my car in a neighbor's garage. We all knew it was going to be a long few days, but the girls and I were safe for the night.

The next day, Dr. Bob called to tell me that a distraught John had called him. It seemed Natalie was upset about everything she had learned about John and said she wanted an abortion. John asked Dr. Bob to meet him at the mall to discuss this mess further. To Bob's surprise when he arrived, Natalie was there with John, and John now had a new twist to share.

Faced with the reality of losing his new life and likely seeing no way to spin what he had done, he returned to his old tricks. First, he said that Dr. Bob and I were having an affair and conspiring against him. He told his fiancée that everything we had told her was a lie and that she shouldn't believe us. I am sure that John's girlfriend really wanted to believe this new narrative, but in the end it wasn't adding up for her. She went to the hospital administration and had John lose his job there and kicked him, our dogs, and his belongings out of her house. It wouldn't be long before John started going after her with threats of custody and defamation.

I appreciated knowing what was happening in John's life, because sometimes when John was feeling frustrated about something, it would result in him lashing out at me. I did feel like I was always a little on edge, but it helped to know when a new terror might be coming. On January 12, 2001, after the breakup with his fiancée, that's exactly what happened. John called me out of the blue and told me that I had to take the dogs back or he was going to euthanize them. He had probably given up his place to live in Ohio and had nowhere to house them after Natalie kicked him out. I couldn't take them back, and he knew that.

I was trying to work, care for the girls, keep the house spotless for showings, and find a new place to live. It was too much. John told me that if I didn't take them back, he was going to have to put them to sleep. It was the last thing I wanted, but I had to stand firm. I told John that that was on him and that he was going to have to look those sweet dogs in the eyes, knowing this was all his fault.

He also told me that he was going to be working a new job during the week and wanted the girls on Saturday and Sunday. I told him again that we already had a visitation schedule, and he couldn't just change his time with them on a whim. Like we had talked about before, he'd have to go back to court and request a change in his visitation schedule. We weren't just on standby.

He used that same phone call to tell me that reporting him to the police was going to cost him his career. I don't think he fully realized how long I had been in frequent communication with the police and the DEA, using what I knew about being a nurse anesthetist to help them build their case against John. Just a few weeks earlier I had spoken to Detective Parker specifically about how the vials John was stealing would have serial numbers on them—distinct numbers that could be traced back to the facility they were taken from. By now I knew that I too had access to the same drugs and it had to at least be something the police were considering.

"You wrote your own story, John."

Any sympathy I once had for him drained from my body. It was strange to see John through such a different lens. His life was falling apart, and in some cases I think I knew about the problems heading his way before he did. But now, instead of seeing him as someone who had overcome so much, I saw him as a person who created chaos for himself and others.

Oddly enough, as I settled into dealing with John and his threats, the people around me seemed to become more on edge. One evening, my friends begged me to come to happy hour at their place. I declined, but they were persistent, and I eventually gave in. Committing to the fun evening out, I left my pager at home. And somehow—I still don't know whether it was me or one of the girls—our phone had accidentally gotten knocked off the hook.

The DEA agent had paged me, but I didn't receive it, of course. I was out for the night. Concerned about not hearing from me, he contacted Detective Parker, who drove out to my house to check on me. Fortunately, the neighbors knew where I was and had him call me at my friend's house. It was nice to feel so protected, but it was also a chilling reminder that this wasn't a normal or even a contentious separation. I was in very real, constant danger, and this detective knew it.

By the middle of January, Natalie had found the drugs John had been hiding in her house, and that was the last straw. She no longer wanted anything to do with him. I knew John would be looking for someone to blame, and I seemed to be at the top of his list lately. When I heard this from Natalie, I was worried again for our safety. Without his fiancée keeping him in Michigan, it seemed likely he would come back to Ohio.

But on January 20, 2001, I received two surprising phone calls. Even though I already had a sense of how bad things had gotten, they made me realize just how desperate John had become. The first call was from John in the morning. The second was from his former fiancée later that evening.

When John called around 8:00 a.m., he sounded depressed. He apologized for all that he had done and said that he wanted me to go with him to counseling. He asked me if I was sure we should get divorced, and I told him I was. Despite all of the pain he had caused me, I didn't revel in telling him this. I knew he was struggling, and it's hard to watch anyone battle demons like John did. But I also knew without any doubt that he had lied to me our entire lives together and there was nothing he could say or do that would make me even consider taking him back.

Even though I had firmly declined his offer to reconcile, he said that he would do anything and everything to "make things right." I told him that his words meant nothing to me and that his actions in the future would be the only way he could redeem himself. Still working to win me over, he told me that I was a great wife and a wonderful mother, and that he had no idea why he gave it all up. He ended our call, apparently still trying to make amends. He said that he would send me the money that he owed me.

In the evening, I was paged to a 517 area code. When I called the number, I was connected to John's now former fiancée. She said that he had called her at seven that morning to rehash their relationship and attempt to reconcile. She agreed that he sounded depressed and told me that he had threatened suicide.

John had left a duffle bag at her house, and she looked through it. She found syringes labeled as fentanyl. Neither of us was surprised by anything anymore. We compared notes and stories for about an hour. We went over dates and discussed all of John's ridiculous lies, including John's claim that Abby was not his. I learned that John had woven quite a sympathetic tale for her, talking about how he was embarrassed to go to work because everyone there knew that his wife was pregnant by someone else.

Talk of Abby naturally led to the thoughts she was having about her own child, fathered by John. She said she had decided to keep her baby and deny that she knew who the father was. She wouldn't list him on the birth certificate. When she told John her plans, he threatened to take her to court for visitation, and she didn't know how serious he was. After all, if he could walk away from any financial responsibility, why wouldn't he?

She was again apologetic and said that if she could do anything for me, I should call her. I told her that my attorney would probably want to speak with her, but all I really needed from her was her willingness to tell the truth in court.

As John's personal life crumbled, the investigation into his crimes continued on. On January 25, I met with Ron Head and another agent from the DEA. We talked for nearly two hours, and I tried to recall everything I knew about John. They asked me to provide all the information I could about John's doctors, friends, and medical insurance so that they could track as much of his activity as possible. For the first time, I also provided an estimated timeline of all of his deceptions. The agents felt a historical investigation—a deep investigation into John's past actions—would take up to a year to complete. Although the second agent appeared to be dozing off during this interview, I did firmly believe that now someone was going to be tracking John and that he would be arrested.

CHAPTER 13

WIRETAP

If those aren't threats, I don't know what is.

—MIAMI TOWNSHIP POLICE OFFICER, LISTENING TO JOHN'S VOICEMAIL MESSAGES

The end of January brought another big change. John and I had sold our house, and I was officially looking for a new place to live. While the idea of moving was stressful, looking at houses was enjoyable. I set out to find a new place for my fresh start with the girls.

John didn't seem to be experiencing the same sense of peace. He called the afternoon we officially sold our house to tell me that he felt like a "real shit" after signing the papers. He again was very apologetic and said he wanted to keep our family together. His latest idea was for me and the girls to move to Florida with him. He was clearly trying to isolate me from my family and everyone I knew.

I told him he needed to see a counselor.

Truly, at this time, I don't think I fully understood just how irredeemable John was. I knew without a doubt that I no longer wanted to be married to him, and I worried about him spending time with the girls. But I didn't yet understand that, as a psychopath, therapy wouldn't help him. So I told him to see a psychologist if he really wanted to make any positive changes for himself and his children.

As we talked, he again denied using or sending drugs, which was bizarre because he had already admitted to sending drugs to Dan. Frustrated, I told him that I had talked to his ex-fiancée and that I knew he had been threatening suicide. He quickly denied that, but he was also very interested in when we talked. I'm sure he hadn't anticipated that the two of us would learn he had called us both the same morning with the hope of reconciling.

On February 27, 2001, Ellen and I went to the courthouse for what was supposed to be a hearing for our divorce, but it had been changed to a contempt hearing because I had recently refused to let the girls go with John for one of his scheduled visits. I was nervous, of course, but I was prepared to explain that I hadn't felt it was safe to send the girls with him. It ended up not mattering—the start time of the hearing came and went, and John was nowhere to be found.

Eventually, John called the courthouse to explain his delay. He said he had been in a car accident and had hit his head. He did arrive, but he was an hour and a half late. He looked disheveled and out of sorts. His pant leg was tucked into his sock, as if he had dressed in a rush. Suspicious of his story, my dad immediately went out to check his car, which had no marks on it.

We went ahead with the hearing, and Detective Parker was first on the stand, but he didn't want to give any specific testimony about evidence he had collected or the ongoing investigation. He did testify that he was working in conjunction with the DEA and the Santa Cruz, Dayton, and Springboro police departments to investigate John. He also testified that I was not under any investigation.

John testified that he was doing locums work in Michigan but was applying for a job in Indiana outside of Fort Wayne. He did not know the name of the hospital or what his schedule would be. We wanted to demonstrate that he was all over the place—being investigated, changing jobs, moving from state to state—and Ellen's carefully delivered questions did just that.

John refused to make a list of what he wanted from the house, so the court decided that we would meet at the house on March 10, toss a coin, and pick in turn until all property was divided. I felt sick to my stomach knowing that we would have to spend an entire day together at the house. I was also suspicious that he just wanted to get into the house because there were still drugs or money hidden there.

Before we picked through our joint property, we each had to submit a list of property we considered personal or owned prior to marriage and exchange it for review. If anything was disputed, it was to be put in storage at the shared expense of both of us. I pointed out that John already had two computers that he had taken from our house, so he was given a choice to return the computers so that they could be part of what we picked on the 10th or keep them and give me the first two picks in the house. He chose to keep the computers, and I was so disappointed. I really wanted to get my hands on those computers and would have traded any furniture to do so.

John arrived at the house for our court-mandated division of property. Both of my parents and Mr. Schikner were there to support me. A detective and two uniformed police officers were present, thanks to Detective Parker's insistence. I thought John was supposed to arrive with a moving van and people to help him. Instead, he showed up late in his BMW with our two dogs.

The officers stopped John in the driveway to set the tone for the day. And I'm sure John was surprised to see the police at all. I can only imagine how angry he was to see them.

When he came into the house, I reminded him about the computers and that I was to get the first two picks even before the coin toss. He claimed not to have any idea what I was talking about and asked if I had it in writing. I didn't have anything, but I told him I didn't need it in writing. There were plenty of witnesses in the courtroom that day. He could give me the first two picks or leave.

Making a show of what he felt was me being unreasonable, he left the house. I reached for the phone to call my attorney, and the detective came back to the house. He said John had changed his mind and would give me the first two picks. I also won the coin toss. The whole day was embarrassing and uncomfortable.

I had already decided that everything could be replaced except for the items on my list, and John didn't dispute anything I had listed, other than requesting half of the girls' baby books. I disputed a few things on John's list, like the diamond out of my engagement ring, a big-screen television, the radio, the phone, a radar detector, and the towing package in my car.

After most everything was picked, the cops left because things were civil. Mom and I were helping John take things out of the house because he hadn't brought any helpers or packing supplies. When my mom and I were alone in the basement with

John, he pulled a tax law book off the shelf and told us that maybe we should read it. I told him we didn't want to hear any of his crap. I said that if he didn't stick to why he was there—the division of our property—I'd call Detective Parker and he would come and ask John to leave.

He said, "What, are you fucking him?"

"Right, John," I responded, exasperated.

"You always liked guys with little dicks."

"Yeah, I married you!"

My mom and I went upstairs and told Dad and Mr. Schikner what John had said in the basement. My dad stewed about it for a while and then confronted John in the foyer. The confrontation turned into a yelling match and Mr. Schikner had to pull my dad away from John.

John left to take some things home, and when he came back, he filed a report with the police stating that my dad had assaulted him, putting his finger on John's chest. I called 911 to get the cops back to the house so that John couldn't manipulate the situation any further. In the meantime, my mom and I worked tirelessly to get all of John's items into the driveway so that we could close the door and leave. We made John go through the house with one of the cops and say that he was satisfied that he had retrieved everything that he wanted. We closed the garage door and left.

I was also still in contact with John's mother, hoping that she would help with the custody case. I knew that she would be a compelling witness, but I also knew that she had more insight into who John really was than anyone. I prayed that she'd be willing to stand up for us, so when I got the following email shortly after John and I divided our assets, I was crushed.

Dear Tonia,

So sorry that the divorce was such a terrible War of the Roses. I feel deeply for both of you. The main reason I have stayed away is that it seems everything I say you use it against John and now you have involved him with Dan's Death somehow with this investigation. Truly what do you hope to gain by this? I have lost a wonderful son and nothing can bring him back. Your anger against John is one thing but to drag this to the point of unresolved closure for me and my family is another thing.

You know dear, you are doing to John what you hated that which he did to you. Your anger is spilling over not only to me, Karen and now your little children. You must let it go. It's over, John is what John is don't destroy yourself too.

Once the divorce is over I would be willing to sit down and talk things over with you. I am sorry for your pain but I have mine, too. Love, Dolores

In March, John's visitation guidelines were changed. Going forward, there would be no restrictions on his time with the girls, as we had requested, because we were concerned that he was a flight risk. Their time with John was also changed to accommodate his new work schedule. One silver lining—John requested to take Emily to California to meet his mother and to purchase a headstone for his brother's grave, but his request was denied.

John's visitations were filled with small issues, but nothing that anyone could do anything about. He was two and a half hours late for his first scheduled time with the girls, and that would soon prove to be normal. He would cancel scheduled visitations at the last minute, which may have been inconvenient at times, but it meant they would be safe with me. The girls just rolled with the schedule changes, and I was always glad to have more time with them. When he'd ask to change his visitation days, it was a little more challenging, but I tried to accommodate him when I could. Making visits easy for John seemed like the best way to make sure Emily and Abby were safe and cared for when they were with him.

Emily would tell me terribly inappropriate things John would share with her, like that I called the police so that he would get into trouble. The girls would come back from a visit with him and their clothes would be filthy, they'd be missing a shoe, and it would be clear they hadn't bathed since I had last had them. I didn't really have any way of knowing how well they were eating or how safe their environment was, but at this point, there wasn't anything substantial enough to report to the courts. And Emily, who did talk about her time with John, didn't indicate that she didn't want to see him or that she felt unsafe with him. I didn't have to pry, because Emily would come home with a pretty full report.

I still heard from John's ex-fiancée occasionally. Most recently she had shared that John had been harassing her with increased intensity. She had already spoken with the District Attorney's Office to file a complaint. John had issued a new and creative threat. He was going to put flyers containing explicit sexual information about her on people's windshields outside of the hospital where she worked. He threatened to report her brother to his place of work, telling them that he had been arrested for possession of marijuana. He said he was going to go for full custody of their child because she was unfit. The list was so bizarre, and it seemed to just go on and on. She wondered out loud if her life would ever be normal again. Eventually, she would be so scared by John's threats, she would decline to testify on my behalf as I had hoped she would. She had to put the safety of her family first.

By mid-May, John and I had settled into a routine of exchanging messages about spending time with the girls—an early pick-up here, an extra day there. I knew he wasn't at risk of earning Father of the Year, because he canceled visits often, and when he had the girls, he'd often leave them with someone else for much of his visitation time. We had been required by the magistrate to complete a psychological evaluation for parenting time, and I was the only one who had taken the necessary steps to complete her request. John remained in the girls' lives, and they looked forward to seeing him.

In one of our conversations, John mentioned that he was moving to Indiana the next day. I asked him why he was moving and, more importantly, if he had considered how Emily and Abby would feel about him being so far away. As usual, he hadn't given the situation any thought and had no real answer, other than the fact that he said he had the "quintessential" job, making $130,000 a year doing nothing.

My response was, "Once again, you choose money over family."

A few days later, John called and wanted to know if he was going to get the kids that weekend. Thinking he had moved, as he said he would, I asked him where he was thinking he'd see them.

"Indiana," was his immediate, one-word reply.

I told him that I was not going to let them leave the state until he was no longer under investigation.

"Am I still under investigation?" he asked.

I wasn't sure if he was being serious or snarky. I told him I didn't know, but that he should call them and confirm.

A dark cloud seemed to come over him at that point. He told me that I should call his mother and confirm his family's mafia ties. A little taken aback, I told him they had already told me all about it.

"So you know it's true?"

I said that I did, still more thrown by his sudden change in mood than by the threat of his mafia ties.

He went on to explain, "Because when this is over, that is when it is going to happen."

As much as I had gotten used to John's bullying tone and violent threats, this felt different. Plus, I was in the habit of writing down, recording, and reporting everything that happened with John as soon as it occurred. So as soon as I got off the phone with John, I called Detective Parker and left him a voicemail.

Parker had me call the Miami Township police since I was now living outside of his jurisdiction. They had me get a wiretap for my phone and an external recording system from RadioShack. They also offered to have someone in the area when the children were exchanged. The officers I worked with seemed very concerned, and I appreciated their commitment to our safety. I was also glad they were so specific in their instructions. Who knows how to install a wiretap on their phone line and set up recording systems? I never imagined I'd need to know that kind of information.

I bought the equipment, set it up, and began recording all of our conversations. I no longer had to take so many detailed notes about when John called and what he said. I also have those recordings to look back on, and they still give me chills today. The following journal entries are equally haunting, so simple some of the time and terrifying at others.

> *Saturday, June 16*
>
> *Went to work picnic. Got home around 11 pm and received 2 messages…2 heated messages stating that he knew that I contacted the Indiana Board. He told me to 'sleep well'. I returned his call and asked him what his problem was and he said that he was smiling because in so many words he was going to have me done. He told me to enjoy the time I have left on this earth because I had 'Fucked him over for the last time." At first, he said that he would be in Bermuda with a 22 year old and taking care of the children himself then later he stated that they would be with my parents wondering, "Gee, what happened to Mom?" I immediately called Miami Township police and filed a report.*
>
> *Sunday, June 17*
>
> *Had officer here to supervise pick up of girls. Officer left at 10:22. I told the officer that I wanted to leave the house after 30 minutes was up because I didn't want John to show up here unannounced without an officer. I called John's home # and there was no answer. I called Ellen at*

> *10:30 to say that he was a no show. Left house at 10:40. Returned at 12:15 and he had left Barbie car at door. No note, no call.*

On June 22, 2001, Miamisburg Court issued a warrant for the threatening messages he had left and asked me to come in that day for a temporary protection order (TPO). They needed to know when he was scheduled to see the girls again. With his move to Indiana, I had to tell them I really didn't know, but I would do what I could to find out.

On June 27, I was back in court again, but this time it was at John's request. And this time, there was definitely more happening behind the scenes than John knew about.

John requested six weeks of uninterrupted visitation that would include a trip to California. He also wanted to be allowed to bring the girls to Indiana, where he was now living, and have access to the college savings account my dad had set up for Emily.

I'm not sure if John forgot or didn't know, but he had a warrant out for his arrest in Montgomery County. Even though our court appearance was in Warren County, Detective Parker let Montgomery County officers know when John would be at the Warren County courthouse, and that they could meet us there and arrest him. I would even get to witness his apprehension.

The Montgomery County officers confirmed his warrant and met us at the courthouse. They told me to stretch when I saw John come in the door.

Fifteen minutes after our scheduled court appearance, Ellen told me that John had been in a minor traffic accident and was delayed in filing a report. We had a good laugh since he had used this excuse for being late once already. But then

I wondered if he was going to luck out again and avoid being arrested that day.

John did still come to the courthouse, arriving a little more than an hour late. He went straight to the bathroom and then to the office to inform them that he was there. John's attorney came out and let him know that the hearing had been canceled because he was so late. From across the room, I could see that John looked upset and then tossed some papers at his attorney—probably his accident report.

John's attorney was then called to the info desk and was notified that officers were there to arrest his client. John had about ten minutes with his attorney, then they walked together toward the front door. They were greeted by the police, who spoke briefly with John before escorting him away from the building. We left. He was not handcuffed or frisked. It was a bit anticlimactic.

For what it's worth, we drove to where John was parked to look at his BMW. It did have some front-end damage, so it seems John really was having a bad day.

I heard from Christy, my crisis counselor and court advocate who was assigned to me once I requested the temporary protection order, that John's bond was set at $100,000, but that he was released on his own recognizance. We talked about getting the CPO and she told me that John's attorney had already filed a motion to amend the TPO to remove the girls.

On July 2, we had additional depositions. I didn't see John's car in the lot, but I waited in a grocery store parking lot across the street anyway, so that Ellen and I could walk in together. John was already there, so I was glad I waited. It was more proof that I should keep following my gut.

First, Ellen deposed John, who admitted that he had quit his job in Indiana a month before and hadn't worked since. He then started in on his lies. He claimed that his mother was paying his bills while he put together a lawsuit against me for defamation of character. The lawsuit, he explained, would be based on his presumption that I had asked someone to report him to the Indiana Board of Nursing in an attempt to discredit his character and keep him from obtaining his license.

He went on to say that he was also taking care of his brother's kids because they were teenagers and were having teenager trouble in the wake of their father's death. Continuing with the idea that he was a model paternal figure, he described how he was getting the girls' room ready in Indiana and that he was in the process of determining paternity of his ex-fiancée's baby so that he could file for full custody. John provided a long list of what he wanted and why—and we didn't even finish his deposition that day. We put a follow-up meeting on the books for later in July.

At this point, every time I saw John, he seemed to look worse. At the last deposition, his hands were shaking and his face was pale. I assumed it was due to his continued drug use, but the more I learned about what was happening in his life, the more I thought it was likely also stress. Ellen had called John's ex-fiancée, hoping she would come in for a deposition, and learned that he was in court with her as well for custody and visitation of their new baby.

I met with a new detective at the Miami Township Police Station and gave him the recording of the threatening messages John had left me. We talked for about thirty minutes, and by the time I got home, he had already left a message saying, "If those aren't threats, I don't know what is." His message also said that he would take them to the prosecutor in the morning and get back to me.

On July 9, I completed paperwork for a civil protection order (CPO) ex parte, meaning it was an emergency order and that John didn't have to be notified of my request for it to be granted. We continued with our deposition, only this time I was the one primarily being deposed. The questions were pretty standard, but one really stood out.

John's attorney—at John's direction, I am sure—asked me if I knew who may have contacted the Indiana Board of Nursing and reported John's previous employment issues. I answered honestly and said yes, but I wanted to keep that name anonymous. Ellen confirmed that I had to answer, so with a knot in my stomach, I told them Jane Parker had reported John. They requested her address and phone number.

Jane was a close friend and an anesthesia classmate. When I told her that John was working in Indiana, she was like, "Hell no." Her family was from and living in Indiana and she decided immediately to call the Indiana Board of Nursing to inform them of John's investigation in Ohio. I think asking for her address was meant to do one of two things: intimidate her or make it seem like they would sue her for defamation or something. I was very scared for Jane, and she took extra precautions to stay safe. Now she had to be looking over her shoulder all the time, worried he would somehow make her life miserable.

Life outside our court battle went on like normal, and one day I ran into an old friend I hadn't seen in a decade. When I told her John and I were divorcing, she told me she was still friends with one of John's old law school roommates from UD, Kevin. He had told her that John was a con artist back when they were in college. Why hadn't he warned me?

Kevin and I connected and spoke at length. He told me more about John's past, all of which was appalling, but nothing was surprising anymore. He told me that John had flunked out of law school; he hadn't left because of his loans not processing in time as he'd falsely claimed. He had taken out multiple credit cards in other people's names. He was cheating on me while we were engaged. Some things I knew and some I had suspected.

Because Kevin now worked for the FBI, he ran John's Social Security number before we connected. He found that John had used several variations of his Social Security number. Like so many others, he said he was concerned about the threats and would help me in any way he could.

Back in mediation with John, we had a very significant discussion—child support. It was clear when looking at John's bank statements that he had moved nearly $30,000 from his accounts, presumably to decrease his overall worth and lower his child support payments. But his plan didn't work, because payments were determined based on his average income from the previous three years, so he was still ordered to pay $2,300 a month for Emily and Abby's care.

We talked about other property, some of which seemed standard, and some of which seemed strange. John was ordered to pay me $4,000 (half of his tax return), and he never did. I was awarded the Jeep we had purchased as a married couple. John continually asked for—of all things—a gold coin I was given as a gift on my twenty-first birthday, before we had even met. Was he fixating on these strange requests as some kind of technique to distract me? I don't think I'll ever really know.

That day, we worked with our attorneys—dug through all of the details of our lives—for eight hours. I still don't know how it could have taken that long. Looking back at my notes, two things give me chills. First, I was reminded of John's behavior.

John's attitude was that this was all funny. He would throw his head back and start laughing if we looked at him.

I'm sure it was meant as an intimidation tactic, but my attorney and I both found it more ridiculous than anything else. It was unsettling to a certain degree, but I don't think it was for the reasons John intended. The man I knew now—the real John Meehan—was not the man I thought I had married. That growing realization, more than any posturing from him going forward, was what terrified me. I simply didn't know what he would do next, but I had finally accepted that nothing was off-limits.

> *The Bank one account was ordered to be put into the existing Merrill Lynch accounts and no money could be removed without both signatures. I insisted that in the event of my death a second signature would still be needed.*

When I read, in my own words, that I had insisted on a second signature to withdraw money from that account in the event of my death, I was reminded that, during these proceedings, I was operating with the knowledge that John wouldn't hesitate to kill me if it served his purpose.

In September of 2001, I learned that John had never attended a single meeting for his psychological evaluation that had been ordered by the family court. When pressed, he said he didn't complete the sessions because he had been visiting his mother and handling family business. He also shared that his mother had apologized to him for some of the things she had done wrong when he was younger, and the two had reconciled. I knew she had been calling John's ex-fiancée on his behalf, and that she had reached out to me recently, though we hadn't connected, so it seemed like this could be true. Somehow John had convinced her to be on his side again, despite her knowing all of the terrible things he had done.

John went on for so long, we ran out of time again and had to schedule another time to meet. Ellen shared that the magistrate was irritated that the case was going on for so long. Like everyone except maybe John and his lawyer, she felt like one year was long enough. A few days later, Ellen called and said that the magistrate had decided to rule on our case before meeting again. She awarded me full custody and denied John out-of-state visitation until he completed the psychological evaluation. She ordered him to sign the divorce decree, pay child support, and release the funds from the sale of our house. Much to my relief, she also ordered that John's grandfather's gun remain in my possession until the CPO was lifted and that John couldn't have visitation until he completed parenting classes. I felt like I was finally winning.

The magistrate told John that he was a non-credible witness because of the conflicting testimony he offered. She shared examples and really made it a point to explain her ruling. I was relieved, but Ellen warned that they had fourteen days to file objections.

On October 13, John showed up to take the girls and claimed that he didn't know he wasn't able to have his visitations with them until he completed the parenting classes, even though the magistrate's decision had been very clear. He left without Emily and Abby. And then a few days later, as Ellen predicted, John and his attorney filed their objections.

1. He didn't feel he should have to turn over his gun.
2. He didn't feel he should be responsible for paying my attorney.
3. He requested a reduction in child support.

His requests weren't too surprising, and they certainly could have been worse. And in the weeks that followed, we had tense but civil exchanges as needed. For whatever reason, his direct threats seemed to stop. Our interactions were far from perfect, but things had gotten so bad that things like delayed child support, which was stressful and problematic for me, became routine. Thinking about those times today, it's sad to realize how much energy I had to put into protecting Emily and Abby from their own father. When I married John, I thought we'd raise the girls together and worry about normal parenting concerns. Are they eating enough vegetables? Are we in the right school district? Should we be saving more for their college tuition? But less than two years after our second child was born, I was not only raising them alone but actively working with the police to build a case against their father, who I now knew was diverting and using drugs. It was a turn of events I never could have predicted.

One threat he hung onto was that he was going to sue me for slander because he was sure I had encouraged my friend Jane to call the Indiana Board of Nursing to prevent him from becoming licensed in the state. I'm not sure if he kept that threat up because not being able to work in Indiana had caused him so many issues or if it was because he knew how much it hurt me to think of my friends and family being tormented by John. He never did file charges against either of us, though I suspect he tried. But what happened with Jane was simple. She was protecting her family and community from John.

On October 31, 2001, John was back in court, but this time it was for his criminal trial. The Montgomery County district attorney was able to bring a charge of aggravated menacing against John based on the threatening voicemail messages he left me.

John was offered a plea deal to avoid a trial—a reduced charge of menacing. Wisely, considering the evidence, he accepted by pleading no contest. He received a thirty-day suspended jail sentence and one year of probation and was required to complete a one-day anger management class.

The result of John's trial was disappointing, to say the least. The court system was new to me, and I really thought an aggravated menacing charge, even as a first offense, would have had more severe consequences. I felt like I was spinning my wheels. We had proof that he had threatened my life, and his punishment was essentially that he had to attend a class for a day.

A small consolation was that John continued to deteriorate physically. He looked thin and sickly sitting in the courtroom. I was still terrified to see him, but I showed up to court to look him in the eye so that he would know that I wouldn't fold. I would protect my kids and myself. And people showed up to court with me—friends and family—showing John that I had even more than just my own strength to get me through whatever he planned to throw at me next.

John had regular visitations with the girls, including what would have been our eleventh wedding anniversary and then Thanksgiving. Drop-offs and pick-ups were hard, and the girls demonstrated a variety of emotions—sometimes fine to see John leave, sometimes crying and asking him to stay, and sometimes upset that he wasn't there at bedtime to read them stories. It was hard to see them upset, but the fact that they missed him gave me hope that he was spending quality time with them when they were together. When he'd bring them home, they'd often be in dirty clothes or missing their socks, so I worried about how well he cared for them.

As Christmas approached, more changes came our way. While John still didn't look well, it seemed he was working, and Emily informed us, "Daddy has a new girlfriend." Most importantly, the judge ruled on some of the objections John presented. He would have to mail his gun to his mother, and he would have to pay $3,000 in attorney's fees.

The question of child support required a separate hearing. I took the stand for the first time and was questioned only by my attorney about what child support I had received thus far. That was an easy answer, because I hadn't received much. At some point John stopped altogether because he struggled to keep a job. The child support he owed started to rack up pretty fast.

John took the stand and testified that he hadn't paid child support because he had sustained a life-threatening injury, had been admitted to the trauma service at the University of Cincinnati Medical Center, and had been unconscious for one week. He reported that his surgical incision had become infected and had to be left open, which prevented him from working.

Fortunately, the judge didn't find his story about being hospitalized for a week to be a good reason for not paying thousands of dollars in child support and found him in contempt. John was ordered to pay all of the child support he owed me by January 1 or go to jail for ten days.

On December 30, I met with Ellen to look over the final divorce decree. We made a few small changes to the wording, and my divorce from John was finalized at 4:24 p.m. on December 31, 2001. It was the last divorce in Warren County for the year. That day I wrote the following note in my journal, and it still feels true today.

> *I never thought in a million years that I would ever say that I was glad to be divorced, but it is a huge relief. There is absolutely no other way it could be.*

I was no longer legally married to John Meehan, but he was still the father of my children and would always be part of our lives. Even as 2001 closed with some hope, I knew I'd still be fighting for Emily and Abby every day with all of my strength, and it was overwhelming. What I didn't know was that in the very next month, a new detective would take over John's case—and he was as committed to stopping John's drug use and abuse as I was to protecting my family.

CHAPTER 14

WHAT HAPPENS IN MEXICO

I could show you four hundred ways
to steal drugs from a hospital.

—JOHN MEEHAN TO DETECTIVE DENNIS LUKEN

One of the earliest entries in my journal, in 2002, perfectly sums up how things were going in my first year as a single mother of two, recently divorced from a man I would eventually understand to be a psychopath.

> *I worked OT 9.5 hrs. John was on time. Emmy had been sick all day. He brought her home in an XL t-shirt and her underwear and coat. No shoes, no socks, no pants. Keeping in mind it is below freezing and there is ~ 5 inches of snow on the ground. Emmy's homework is again untouched.*

I still worried about the girls when they were in John's care, and exchanges like this sent my anxiety through the roof. He couldn't be charged with neglect, and the girls were still usually excited to see him, but looking at Emily, he clearly wasn't taking care of them like a responsible parent would. I was still working with the police and there was more hope every day that John would be charged with a serious crime soon, but it just didn't feel like enough.

After one of their visits, Emily made a comment that "Daddy's leaving for Mexico in the morning." I hadn't known about the trip, but I wasn't worried about it. He hadn't asked to take the girls, so I really didn't care where he was vacationing. As I prepared to meet with the new detective working on John's case, I had no idea that John's trip to Mexico would kick off a series of events that would ultimately and finally land him in prison.

On January 23, I met with Detective Parker, whom I knew well by this point, Elaine Jones from the pharmacy board, and the new detective on John's case, Dennis Luken. In our two-hour meeting, I heard new stories, learned about new evidence of old crimes, and felt a renewed sense of energy around John's case.

Elaine shared that fentanyl had gone missing from Fort Hamilton Hospital, where John had recently started working, and everyone in the department was asked to give a urine sample. John was the only one who said he couldn't provide a sample. He then asked to go get a cup of coffee. They denied his request initially but eventually let him go. When John returned, he turned in a cold urine sample. Before the medical professionals taking the specimen noticed the temperature, a nurse and security guard came forward and identified John as the man they had just seen taking urine from a patient's Foley bag. When confronted, John fled the hospital and was nowhere to be found for close to a week.

Later, when he attempted to return to work, John claimed to have injured his abdomen while mowing the grass. Knowing what I know now about how John operated, I think he was setting up a lawsuit. John told his employer that he tripped over an exposed cable in his yard and perforated his colon with the lawnmower handle. This had caused air to leak into his abdomen from his colon and was the reason his specimen was cold. He went on to explain that he had left that day because he wasn't feeling well and eventually had to have emergency abdominal surgery to repair the tear. This was, of course, a ridiculous story, but it seemed to be the best John could come up with. He provided them with evidence of the incision, and he knew exactly how to ensure it remained infected, so it was difficult for them to dispute his claims.

In our meeting, Detective Parker provided Detective Luken with pictures of the drug box and all of the vials recovered from our old house. I watched as he put on gloves to pick up and log each vial. He wrote down lot numbers and manufacturer names that he said could potentially be traced to the hospital they were shipped to. Watching him record information, I could see he was meticulous. I was confident he would follow through and dared to feel hopeful. The information he was gathering would prove that the vials came from hospitals where John had worked and I hadn't, making it much more difficult for John to pin the stolen drugs on me.

About a week later, I got a call from a woman named Julie who said she was the best friend of John's new girlfriend, Meg. Julie said that she was worried about Meg and that something just didn't seem right about him.

Does he work for the Justice Department? Is he a doctor? Did he finish law school? She peppered me with questions and I gave her honest answers, none of which made her feel better.

Julie said that Meg had been dating John for about three months and that they had just gone to Mexico together. While there, John began complaining about back pain and had to be admitted to the hospital. Meg opted to fly home without him, and Julie was suspicious that there was more to the story. She asked if I'd talk to Meg, and I said I would.

Julie was right—there was more to Meg's story than she had shared. John did tell her that he was a doctor, but what had concerned her was that, while they were on vacation, he was giving himself IV medications. I told her to contact Detective Luken.

Meg connected with Luken and shared even more information. On two occasions, John had asked her for urine specimens, claiming that patients undergoing anesthesia during a surgical procedure can emit a gas that in turn he could carry home and that could then contaminate her and her children. For a research study and her own safety, he said he needed to test her urine. Though it seemed odd, she had agreed.

She also shared that John had still not returned from Mexico and her house cleaner was scheduled to clean John's house the next day. Seeing this as an opportunity, Detective Luken advised her to contact him if the cleaner found any vials of drugs used in anesthesia in John's home. Meg agreed, and since she had heard John access the attic in the bathroom before and was suspicious that he may be hiding things there, she instructed the cleaner to be sure to look there.

Detective Luken reached out to Captain Alan Laney at the Fairfield Township Police Department, in the jurisdiction where John resided. He advised Captain Laney that he may be contacting him for assistance with executing a search warrant on John Meehan's residence the following day.

Detective Luken and Captain Laney responded to the residence, and Meg showed them the drugs she had found in the attic. They immediately left the residence and returned to the Fairfield Township Police Department. Captain Laney and Detective Luken drafted a search warrant, brought Meg to the judge's office, and had her swear to the information contained in the affidavit for the search warrant.

Once the search warrant was signed, Luken and Laney went back to John's house, executed the search warrant, and seized the bag Meg had found. Upon examination, they discovered that the bag contained empty vials, syringes, and other miscellaneous drugs. A partial list from Detective Luken's report of the drugs in John's house included: thirty empty vials of Versed, four empty vials of fentanyl, six empty vials of Demerol, and three empty Carpujects, which are pre-filled delivery systems, of meperidine, which is the generic name for Demerol. They also recovered a Ruger 9mm semi-automatic pistol, the exact gun I had told the Springboro police he had when they searched his car. John having that in his home was a violation of the terms of his probation.

Luken then aggressively continued the investigation on his own, all while John was still in Mexico. He contacted John's recent employers and reviewed with them the drugs that had been removed from John's house, now fully researched and organized on a spreadsheet. He was able to confirm that the information from the drug vials and ampoules recovered from John Meehan's residence was consistent with information from drug vials and ampoules at a hospital in Maysville, Kentucky.

Detective Luken also spoke with a doctor at Meadowview Regional Medical Center in Maysville. The medical team there found a twenty-seven-gauge syringe and a vial of Demerol behind a Pyxis automated dispensing machine located in the operating room. The syringe contained bloody residue, which meant it potentially contained DNA, and presumably John's DNA. They still had the syringe and vial evidence secured in their facility, so it could be tested. Luken reached out to the Commonwealth's Attorney's Office for the county and spoke with a prosecutor, but he declined to aid in the investigation unless and until the hospital filed a report. But the hospital didn't want to file a report or draw any attention to the incident. Working with the prosecutor's office had the potential to lead to bad press for the hospital or lawsuits by patients who could claim to have received substandard care from a drug addict.

On February 1, John returned from Mexico. Meg still had John's car, keys to his house, and some of his personal items. She let him know that she would leave the car for him at the airport so that he could drive it home. She ended up running into John at the airport and told him things between them were over but didn't indicate that she had discovered anything about his drug use.

I had a bad feeling that John might come by my house, so I took the girls to a friend's place for the night. I went back to my home, but I camped out in my car, so that I could watch my own house. Sure enough, John came by around six but didn't stay long. I went to visit a friend for the evening and came home around ten. John hadn't called or left any kind of message.

The next time I heard from Meg, I learned that John had contacted her on February 2, begging her to marry him, and when she declined, he called a few days later threatening suicide. I told Meg that this was a very familiar routine.

Detective Luken continued his investigation and was able to determine that none of the drugs found in John's possession came from my hospital, eliminating me as a suspect, but also preventing John from claiming that I was as likely to be a source of the drugs found as he was. Now John couldn't say I was framing him. It was so reassuring to see how much faster this new detective could get things done. I had renewed confidence that justice in my case would prevail.

As part of standard procedure, John was made aware of what had been seized from his house when he wasn't home, including the gun, which was his most immediate problem. On February 11, 2002, John was sentenced to thirty days in jail for violating his probation by possessing a firearm.

Luken attempted to interview John at the jail, but John invoked his right to counsel. Even though he couldn't interview John, Luken was still on his case. He contacted the Montgomery County Detention Facility where John was being held and provided the supervisor with information about John's drug addiction. He predicted that John would falsely claim to be suffering from a health problem in order to receive pain medication for his addiction. Even though Luken had called as soon as he could, the supervisor at the jail told him that it was too late. John had already claimed that he fell out of the top bunk and injured himself. He had been given pain medication.

Detective Luken, whom I had started calling Denny, was not giving up on stopping John. On February 12, Denny attempted to meet with John about the drugs recovered at his residence. John invoked his right to counsel again, but then said, "I could show you four hundred ways to steal drugs from a hospital."

Nearly a week later, with his lawyer present, John met with Denny and Elaine Jones at the Montgomery County Detention Facility. John's attorney stated he would be willing to admit to stealing drugs from one of the hospitals if they agreed not to pursue criminal charges for theft in other jurisdictions. On March 1, John entered a plea of guilty to one count of theft of drugs. He also agreed to enter an inpatient drug rehabilitation program.

On March 5, John showed up to a detox program, claiming not to have used any drugs for the previous seven weeks. Because he denied having a drug problem, the facility wouldn't accept him. He then went to the Ohio State University Hospital and faked a back injury so that he could receive Demerol. Once he was using again, he went back to the rehab program and admitted to using. John was then allowed into the drug detox program.

While John was supposed to be in the detoxification process, he continued to report that he was in pain and was transferred to a hospital in Columbus, Ohio. Because he knew exactly what to say to the medical professionals treating him, he undoubtedly received pain medication. John eventually left the program before completing the required twelve weeks. He continued this pattern of reporting pain, going to a hospital, and receiving drugs while in treatment to feed his addiction.

Shortly after signing himself out of rehab, John checked into a hospital in Washington Court House, Ohio, using his deceased uncle's name, John Boles. He claimed to be suffering from kidney stones. Eventually, hospital security noticed that John's 750 BMW had been in the parking lot, unlocked and unmoved, for three days. The car had out-of-county Ohio license plates, so as standard procedure, they sent the plate numbers to the Ohio Bureau of Motor Vehicles (BMV) database to determine the vehicle's owner. It was registered to John, and they quickly found that there was a protection order against him, involving me.

A police officer contacted me and let me know that John's car was in the hospital lot. He said that they had found two IDs in the car: one for John Meehan and one for John Boles. When they inquired about any patients with either of those names, the hospital said that a John Boles was currently admitted.

The officer went to John Boles's room. The patient had been admitted as an attorney, paying cash for his stay at the hospital. There the officer found John Meehan. He asked John why he had a second driver's license in addition to his own. John told the officer that the other ID belonged to his brother.

This officer was quite confused and called me. He asked, "Ma'am, what do we have here?"

I gave a little bit of history and then told him the Washington Court House police needed to call Detective Luken at the Warren County Drug Task Force immediately. When they did, Denny advised them that John was using deception in order to obtain dangerous drugs and then provided them with information as to the appropriate charges to file.

On May 30, when John was released from the hospital, he was immediately placed under arrest by the Fayette County Sheriff's Office and transported to the local jail. Upon John's arrival at the jail, he faked a seizure and was transported back to the hospital where he had been arrested. The hospital refused to readmit him to their hospital, and he had to be transferred to another hospital in Columbus, Ohio.

CHAPTER 15

IT'S A LONG WAY TO THE BOTTOM

Hey Snitch, how's my favorite police informant doing?

—POSTCARD FROM JOHN TO ONE OF HIS VICTIMS, 2005

On June 10, 2002, John appeared in court for sentencing. He had entered a not guilty plea on March 2 of the same year but hadn't yet learned what that would mean for him. The judge sentenced him to six months in a facility for first-time drug offenders, which would be followed by one year of intensive supervision, and then five additional years of probation.

John, as everyone expected, requested a stay on his sentence so that he could arrange care for his dogs and handle a few other responsibilities. The judge denied his request, but she did give him twenty-three hours to report to the facility. She also told him that if he failed to report, the consequence would be serious—eighteen months in prison.

We now know that, after John left the courthouse, he didn't focus his energy on making arrangements for the time he'd be spending in treatment. Instead, he drove to Michigan, to three different hospitals where he had previously worked as a nurse anesthetist. Using his identification badge, he signed out anesthesia boxes full of controlled substances from as many of the hospitals as he could.

John then drove to an inexpensive hotel and paid cash for one night, telling the hotel clerk that he may stay longer. He hung a "Do Not Disturb" sign on his door and wasn't seen by anyone until the next day.

When a hotel employee saw the Do Not Disturb sign still on John's door after the checkout time had passed and confirmed that John had not paid to stay another night, he knocked. When there was no answer, he had the front desk call John's room. When there was still no answer, he assumed that John had simply left without checking out, so he tried to open the door.

He could only get the door open a few inches, but it was enough to see a man lying on the floor of the room. He tried calling out to the man, and when he didn't receive a response, he had the front desk call paramedics.

When police and paramedics arrived and gained access to the room, John was in a semi-conscious state and able to answer some of their questions. He was shaking and unsteady on his feet, but he could tell them his name, his vehicle information, and some details about what had happened the night before, explaining why he was found passed out in a room that was in disarray.

Looking around the room, the officers and paramedics could see a gray box, a blue vinyl bag, open and unopened unmarked vials, a small vial of Demerol, and a syringe with liquid and blood in it. Using what they could see as a starting point, they tried to get John to explain to them what was happening.

According to police reports, one of the officers directly asked John if he had been using any of the drugs that were strewn about the room—and, despite the risk to his own health, John lied, emphatically saying, "Absolutely not." John claimed to be fine, and that he was just disoriented because he had fallen asleep on the floor and was having trouble waking up. He went on to say that he was an anesthetist, and that he had worked late the night before and hadn't had any place to dispose of the empty vials and syringes in the room, so he was going to take them to work with him that morning and dispose of them there.

The officer also noted about $1,500 in cash in a white envelope sitting on a table in the room. John told the officer that the cash was his paycheck and that he was going to deposit it into his checking account. He also consented to officers searching his car, which was in the hotel parking lot.

Reading the police report, I can only imagine how awkward this conversation must have been. It, of course, makes no sense that John would work late as a nurse anesthetist and not have a place to properly dispose of contaminated medical supplies. But the officer let John keep digging himself into a hole. Finally, he asked why John would bring the anesthesia box, needles, and vials of narcotics to his hotel room, and John didn't have an answer. When asked where he had worked the night before, John told him Tawas Hospital. The officer indicated they would confirm that he had been at the hospital, to which John replied, in still-slurred speech, "Well, [they] may not say that..."

Paramedics continued John's medical examination in the hotel room and found obvious track marks from some type of needle injections on his arms and small, dried blood spots on and around his toes, where it appeared he had also received injections of some kind.

Still monitoring John and attempting to assess his physical health based on the clues in his environment, the paramedics found a bloody washcloth near the bathroom. When they asked John about it, he said, "I had a bloody nose." When they asked about bloody socks they found on the floor, he said, "I was playing basketball last night and got a blister, and it popped."

The image of John's hotel room painted in that police report is horrifying. Syringes, tourniquets, bloody items, and enough anesthesia drugs for multiple surgeries—I can't imagine everything that had to have been going through their minds. And yet, I'm sure they weren't too shocked, since answering calls to help people who have harmed themselves or others is unfortunately a common part of their jobs.

Though I'm sure all the police officers and medical professionals knew that John had been using drugs illegally, they still didn't have the whole picture. What had he taken? When? How much? Even though John had clearly stopped making good decisions for himself, they had to try to help him. The police report reads:

> *MEEHAN was unable to produce any type of identification showing that he was an employee of any hospital in the area. MEEHAN gave this Officer an address in Ohio. While information was being gathered by Medical Personnel, this*

> *Officer checked the gray box that had a number 23 on the top. Also in the blue fannie pack, the number five was observed painted on the vinyl case and also a sticker from St. Luke's Hospital. This Officer also observed a padlock with a key on the keychain with the number 23 and indication stated return to pharmacy.*

Even though John had clearly broken a few laws, the paramedic rightly determined that, because they didn't know which drugs John had administered to himself or when, he had to be taken to a hospital immediately. There was a very real possibility he had overdosed and they were dealing with a ticking clock.

John was loaded into the ambulance without incident and the police officer and paramedic agreed to meet at Covenant Health, where John could get the medical care he needed. Though John was initially compliant, he had other plans.

About five minutes into the ride to the hospital, John unbuckled his safety restraints, grabbed the two anesthesia drug boxes, and jumped out of the moving ambulance.

Police in the area, including the officer still at the hotel, were notified that John had been seen running to the Fashion Square Mall. Multiple officers responded and entered the mall, retrieving clues from store employees and customers as they searched for John. People reported that someone fitting John's description had been seen on the second floor of the warehouse section of JCPenney, frantically attempting to take a comforter from a display. Store security correctly assessed that John was in a dangerous state and didn't engage with him—instead, they passed his location on to the police, who located John standing on top of the elevator car from the warehouse section.

No one knew how John got on top of the elevator, but it was now clearly a dangerous situation. Police attempted to reason with John, asking him to come down so that he could be examined at the hospital. John's response was to begin dropping vials from the boxes he was carrying through the steel grate in the elevator. The vials were sealed, and no one could quite figure out what John was hoping to accomplish.

Suddenly, the officers who had been talking to John lost sight of him, and the only direction he could have gone was up. As John headed up the elevator shaft toward the second floor, officers confirmed that the second-floor elevator doors couldn't be opened due to a safety feature. John would at least be contained in the elevator shaft, even if he still wasn't safe from harm.

The officers on the scene were able to look through a window into the elevator shaft and see that John had climbed up the wall and was standing on top of the second-floor doors. I doubt John realized it, but he was in the perfect spot: They couldn't open the elevator doors because John was standing on them, and they couldn't move the elevator without risking hurting John. Their only option was to try and talk him down.

When the officers tried speaking with him, he refused to leave the elevator shaft and asked for water. By this time, the fire department had arrived and was attempting to reach John through a maintenance hatch, using one of their ladders.

With the ladder positioned next to John, officers continued to try to coax him down, but he insisted that he needed water first. They went back and forth, John angrily insisting that they should throw the water up to him and the officers pointing out that, if they did, he might fall when he attempted to catch the bottle. John was precariously balanced, and it was just too risky.

Because John was so agitated, it was decided that it wasn't safe to climb the ladder and arrest him. They took the ladder down and instead had one of the maintenance personnel begin moving the elevator up, closer to John. When the elevator was about twelve feet below John, two officers climbed into the elevator shaft. John became more frantic and tried to climb farther up the shaft, but there was nothing for him to climb on.

The officers had been trying to coax John into surrendering, but now the tone of the situation had changed. John jumped from a beam onto the motor of the elevator, and it looked to the officers like he was about to pull the wires out and attempt to use them as a weapon. Responding to the urgency of the situation, one officer was able to grab John's right ankle. When John realized the officer had a firm grip, he changed tactics, lowering his body slightly and kicking the officer in the jaw.

Even though the kick landed, it wasn't enough to make the police officer let go. He did, however, step backward into the open trapdoor on top of the elevator car. The officer's commitment to hanging onto John meant John was pulled down with him.

Emergency personnel caught the officer as he dropped into the elevator, while John fell on top of the elevator car, hitting his head on support rods and briefly losing consciousness. He was handcuffed and lowered through the still-open trapdoor.

John was taken to the hospital and treated for minor wounds, and the police officer he had kicked in the face was treated at the scene. Looking around the elevator shaft, police recovered one of the bags of narcotics that John had had in his hotel room and the envelope of cash.

Ultimately, John was charged with Intent to Do Great Bodily Harm Less Than Murder and Unlawful Possession of a Controlled Substance (Narcotic or Cocaine). When he was released from the hospital, he was taken to the county jail. On November 27, 2002, John was sentenced to twenty-one to sixty months of incarceration in the Michigan Department of Corrections.

For at least twenty-one months, I would know where John was, and that he couldn't just show up on our doorstep. I felt such relief. And we enjoyed that peaceful time. John's family sent gifts and cards on birthdays and holidays. We even spoke on the phone a few times, just catching up on how our lives were going. It was clear to me that John's family was very different from John, and they understood, probably from having experienced something similar themselves, just how much harm he had done. One of the most amazing acts of generosity came from John's sister Donna. While John was in prison, she paid his drastically reduced child support payments, in part so that he wouldn't come out of incarceration so far behind in payments, but also because she just didn't feel it was right that the girls and I didn't have financial support from John during that time.

An important shift also happened in my life around this time. I developed a closer relationship with my friend and fellow CRNA, Augie Bales. He and I had known each other for years and had great respect for each other. I knew him to be a reliable and trustworthy nurse anesthetist, and then, as our friendship developed, I learned he was a reliable and trustworthy person.

In 2001, Augie and his wife were divorcing, and he was focused on making sure his kids were happy and healthy while he and his ex-wife figured out the best way to parent. Since we had been friends and coworkers for so long, he knew all about John and how hard I tried to make everything as good as possible for the girls, and we were able to lean on each other for help and advice. One of his daughters was a teenager, and she would babysit my girls. We were there for each other without judgment, and he was a safe person for me to talk to when I needed one. Eventually he became so much more.

In the summer of 2002, Emily entered me in a drawing to win a free gym membership, and when I was selected to receive free trial memberships for myself and a friend, I gave the extra membership to Augie. One day, the girls and I ran into him as we were leaving the gym. Emily had apparently waited long enough for Augie and me to figure out that we shared an attraction for each other and should start dating. She flat-out asked Augie if he'd like to be her dad.

This melted Augie's heart. The more he had heard about John, the more he felt I deserved better. And the more he learned about me, the more he realized I was the exact life partner he was looking for. I was developing the same feelings. He was the opposite of John, and the more I got to know who he really was, the more impressed I was with the strength of his character. I knew I wanted him in my life.

A lot of people have asked me how I was able to date after what happened with John. How could I ever trust my own judgment again? I don't understand exactly how I was able to connect with Augie so deeply, but I do know that from the start, I decided I wasn't going to let John ruin relationships for me. And I am so glad I let Augie into my life.

On December 27, 2003, Augie and I got married. He knew all about John and had, as much as any of us, an idea of what might come our way when he was released. Augie was not only willing to stand with me and the girls against John, but he was also committed to protecting our new family. Much to John's dismay, he would learn that Augie and I had a strong bond and that, as his life continued to crumble, my life flourished.

Me and the girls with Augie in one of our early family photos.

On August 16, 2004, just weeks before John was released, his attorney contacted me and requested multiple visits with the girls while Donna would be visiting in September, in addition to unsupervised visitation and a standard parenting schedule. We responded with a firm "hell no." He hadn't completed any of his psychological evaluations or the other requirements of his release.

After he was released, we went through all of the required processes, including working with a psychologist to ensure that John's reentry into Emily and Abby's lives was handled in the healthiest way possible. A few things stand out to me about that time, other than just the persistent anxiety I felt about what John would do.

First, the psychologist we worked with specifically told us not to keep John from the girls because it was better for them to "find out for themselves that their dad is a dirtbag than to fantasize that he is a great dad they are missing out on because of you." He was confident that John wasn't genuinely interested in a relationship with his daughters and that he would very likely just go away. This was frustrating to hear. I wanted to know why, if that was the likely outcome, we had to go through the motions. We were all doing so well, and I didn't understand why we were being forced into a situation that was sure to fail and harm everyone involved. He convinced me it was the right thing to do, so we went ahead with the plan as he recommended.

John's time with Emily and Abby was supervised, and right from the start he showed us all that he was still operating as a narcissist. In September of 2004, John had a visitation with the girls at our psychologist's office. John asked if he could bring the girls presents, and the psychologist pointed out that it was important to make the visits about their relationship, not gifts. He was told he could bring one gift for each of them, so, of course, he brought an entire garbage bag full of dollar-store toys.

In a twist we weren't expecting, John requested that his first visitation outside of the counselor's office months later—which would be supervised by Augie at John's request—be in his home. We had assumed the visitations would be in neutral locations, like a park or community center. Still adjusting to the situation, we had to assume the request might be some kind of trap and prepare accordingly. Augie, who would be with John and the girls, hid a tape recorder and a switchblade in his pocket. Our friend John Schikner waited outside in his car, ready to help Augie and the girls if needed. I sat at home, feeling like a nervous wreck.

Sharing all these details after the fact, knowing now that John didn't try anything on that first visit, all of our precautions feel a bit dramatic—but John was such a wild card. We had no idea what to expect, and we were all prepared to defend ourselves and the girls to whatever extent necessary.

I also remember that John's most recent girlfriend was there for that first visit. I can't even imagine what she must have been thinking, sitting with her boyfriend while he was being supervised by his ex-wife's husband. She had daughters of her own.

John tried to bend or break the rules of the visitation multiple times. He wanted to bring Emily upstairs to see the hamsters he had bought her, but that was outside of the agreed-upon arrangement. Of course, Emily wanted to see the hamsters, so I'm sure John was delighted that Augie was the one who had to tell her that leaving his sight wasn't allowed. They did agree to go to the Cincinnati Children's Museum, but Augie again had to intercede when John wanted the girls to ride with him. While he didn't argue with Augie, John continually put him in the position of having to enforce boundaries.

Future visitations were certainly less stressful, but I still worried every moment the girls were away from me. We were really fortunate that John's sister Donna supervised some of the visitations as well. When the girls spent time with Donna and John, they often came home with cute new clothes and toys, and I am sure she paid for everything. Donna worked so hard to make the time the girls had with John a positive experience.

After a year, with only three visits under his belt, John requested reduced child support, unsupervised visits, and to take the girls out of state. He shared photos of himself and the girls during one of their visits, attempting to demonstrate that he was deserving of this significant change in our parenting arrangement. When John's request for more parenting time was denied, he never saw the girls again. In the end, the psychologist and I were both right. The psychologist predicted that he would eventually go away, and I predicted that their hearts would get broken.

I also learned that John was lashing out at people who had supported him over the years. I'm not sure what sparked his anger, but in March of 2006, he wrote his mother a scathing email that she later shared with me.

> *Dolores,*
>
> *Please stop asking about me. I know you are still talking to Tonia and giving her information that is still causing problems. Please do not ask Donna about me. There is no reason why you need to concern yourself with me. I don't like you…and you don't like me. I don't want you to have any contact with my children. You don't need to send them anything. They are better off this way. They don't need to know you or the pain that you cause.*
>
> *If Cathy allows me to see little Danny this is no concern of yours. Think of me as dead…which shouldn't be too hard for you to do. Put a picture of me up on your altar and just forget that I'm alive…and I will do the same for you. You have enough problems right now so try to concentrate on those and just leave me out of your little circle for what time you have left.*
>
> *John*

He also eventually turned on Donna, his sister who had gone above and beyond to try to support him. Over the years, she gave him money, a job, and a place to stay—a home he would eventually try to steal from her—not to mention all the time she devoted to supervising his visitations with the girls. She proved how much she valued family, but even she hit her breaking point when John began threatening her, saying that providing him with a place to live and money when he needed it wasn't enough. The final straw was a new victim who reached out to Donna, saying that John had scammed her out of a lot of money. Donna also ended up in court with John and had to cut ties with him completely. She took the chance that he would come after her or her family for revenge. He'd left her no choice—she just couldn't keep supporting him, and she could see now that he was never going to change.

John didn't forget about Meg or Detective Luken either. While he was in prison and then out on probation, he clearly held a grudge. By the end of 2005 and into 2006, Meg had also found herself in some trouble with the law. John found out and started harassing her while she served her time. Between November 2005 and May 2006, John sent five postcards to Meg with the following messages:

> Hey Snitch, how's my favorite police informant doing? Saw your buddy the other day—I must admit…watching him stand there for five hours with his thumb up his ass made me smile. Only one more year—damn, but I bet your kids don't even remember you!
>
> (Postcard was signed: Denny Luken)

> Yo Snitch, missing you tons it warms my heart to think about you sitting in there. There is a God above. Happy Thanksgiving. Kisses.
>
> (Postcard was signed: Det. Luken)
>
> Just a "shout" to my "gangsta" girl. I'd tell you to go to hell but I figure you're already there—at least in your mind, anyway I bet your kids have forgotten you—no great loss. Nice try with the letter to Oney—Guess who's off parole? See you soon! Do you miss me bitch?
>
> How's my poor little—doing? Freedom is sooo tasty… But you would not know about that. Remember Cancun?
>
> (Postcard was signed: D. Luken)
>
> Nice new prison picture—but it doesn't change what you are inside—a police informant & a liar.
>
> (Postcard was signed: Denny)

Meg let Detective Luken know about the postcards, obviously aware of who they were from and what they meant. It was some comfort knowing that John being in California now would make it more difficult for him to physically confront me, the girls, Meg, or Detective Luken. But we all knew he was still a danger to us. And it wouldn't be long before we'd hear from a new victim and a new detective in sunny California, asking us what we could tell them about John Meehan.

WR-U7

Mickey Unlimited Collection

JUST A "SHOUT" TO MY
"GANGSTA" GIRL
I'D TELL YOU TO GO TO
HELL BUT I FIGURE YOU'RE
ALREADY THERE - AT LEAST
IN YOUR MIND, ANYWAY -
I BET YOUR KIDS HAVE FORGOTTEN
YOU - NO GREAT LOSS ☹
NICE TRY WITH THE LETTER
TO O'NEY - GUESS WHO'S
OFF PAROLE?
SEE YOU SOON!
DO YOU MISS ME? BITCH

2

Post Card

FRPC
P.O. BOX 23651
COLUMBUS, OHIO
43223

Postcard John sent to his ex-girlfriend, Meg, when she was in prison.

Another postcard John sent to Meg, again signing as Denny Luken.

CHAPTER 16

IS THIS EVEN A CRIME?

I'll tell you what I am sure of. You're going to get caught. One way or another. It's a mathematical fact. It—it's like Vegas: the house always wins.

—FRANK ABAGNALE JR. IN CATCH ME IF YOU CAN: THE TRUE STORY OF A REAL FAKE

The work that Dennis Luken and his team put into tracking down John and ensuring that prosecutors had what they needed to prosecute him was incredibly meaningful to me for so many reasons. Denny listened to me, believed me, answered my questions, and helped me during a time when not everyone was willing to believe my story. And many people who did believe me didn't want anything to do with me or the girls because they were so afraid of John, they felt they had to steer clear of all of us for their own safety. But fortunately for us, John was prosecuted and eventually went to prison for a little over two years.

In 2013, I got a call from a police officer in California asking about my relationship with John, our legal battles, and the restraining orders I had filed against him. Not surprisingly, John had quickly found himself under investigation again, but this time, it wasn't related to his drug use.

A patrol officer had received a report of a woman in town who was complaining about her ex-boyfriend bothering her. She said that he wouldn't leave her alone and was threatening to extort her. The ex-boyfriend was, of course, John.

Initially, the officer didn't think that what John was doing was necessarily a crime. It was evident that John wasn't a great guy, but it wasn't clear what laws were really being broken within what seemed like a squabble between former lovers. Still, they wanted to help this woman, as she was clearly distressed.

The officer, who happened to be a woman, called John and informed him that he needed to stop contacting his ex-girlfriend. His ex didn't want anything to do with him, she had made that clear, and the officer asked John to honor her request and just leave her alone.

Amazingly, and much to the officer's annoyance, John did not stop harassing his ex-girlfriend. He doubled down and started calling and harassing the female police officer.

Eventually the officer escalated the situation to her detective sergeant and said, "Hey, can you call this guy and tell him to stop bothering me? He needs to stop calling me and stop calling the victim."

The detective sergeant, a man, called John and firmly told him, "Leave them both alone. You've now been told multiple times." Even that follow-up didn't work. Though John never reached back out to the male detective, he continued to harass both the female officer and the female victim.

After a month, the officer who had initially talked to John connected with a new detective, Julia Bowman. Serendipitously, Detective Bowman had just completed a four-hour professional development course about the crime of stalking. To this day, she credits that class for her response to John's case—a case no one else was sure could even be investigated any further.

Like many police officers, Julia hadn't been a victim of many of the specific crimes she would investigate. Without personal experience, investigators learn the details of crimes, perpetrators, and victims in one of two ways: they complete specific continuing education courses, such as classes on stalking or domestic violence, or they learn on the job as they investigate crimes reported to them.

Detective Bowman had been recently promoted to a job working on what's called crimes against persons—and it's exactly what it sounds like—crimes that harm someone's physical person, like assault, rape, or murder. Wanting to learn more about the cases she'd be taking on, Detective Bowman enrolled in a four-hour stalking class just weeks before John's case came across her desk.

"Hey, is there even a crime here?" they asked Detective Bowman. "How would you suggest we deal with this guy?"

Stalking is a crime in all fifty states, and I'm sure the officer knew that. But there are so many ways one person can stalk another, it can be hard to identify if specific actions are considered stalking. Stalking involves a pattern of unwanted, repeated behavior directed at a specific person. It is a crime of power and control that causes a reasonable person to feel fear or emotional distress. Detective Bowman realized that John could be charged with felony stalking and arrested immediately.

When talking to people about stalking crimes, she explains that it's important that police officers know how to ask the victim the right questions. For example, a stalking victim may report seemingly innocuous behavior, like their potted plant that's always on the right side of their front door being moved to the left side of their front door. A police officer's reaction would likely be something like, "Okay, why are you calling the police?"

The stalking victim would probably go on to say, "Oh, I know it's my ex-boyfriend. I know my ex-boyfriend is taking my potted plant from the right side and moving it to the left side of my porch, so I know that he was here. He knows that I know that he's moving my plant."

Again, as Detective Bowman would explain to me and others, unless the police officer is trained to understand stalking behavior, they are probably going to try to solve the immediate and apparent issue—the plant. Get rid of the plant. Move the plant inside. Put up surveillance cameras. Tell your ex-boyfriend to stop moving your plant. All of these ideas solve the issue with the plant, because that's all the victim and officer are talking about. None of those solutions actually help the victim, and the emotional terrorism continues.

What really resonated with me when talking to Detective Bowman was that if police officers know how to work with victims and their support networks to identify a pattern of behavior, they can take action. It takes education and change on both sides. For instance, if we continue with Julia's plant example, the victim could keep a log of every time the plant has been moved from one side to the other over the last thirty days and present that to the police officer. Imagine how different the situation is when they can tell the police, "Every day for the last thirty days, my ex has driven all the way out to my house, moved my plant from the right side of my porch to the left side." Now the police officer can see the pattern of behavior, that the victim is being targeted, and that her stalker is harassing her. With this information, they can more easily identify the proper charges.

Detective Bowman's story stands out to me both as a critical moment in John's engagement with the police and as a story that law enforcement, legal professionals, and anyone working in medicine can learn from. Because she carefully chose to educate herself about crimes she was less familiar with and how the people those crimes affect may report them, she was able to provide the exact direction needed so that the officers who had encountered John could use legal measures to stop him. The more people we have in our community who approach their work like Detective Bowman does, the harder it will be for people like John to torture their victims.

In this situation, John's actions were now crimes against a person, and that meant it became her case. That was good news for the victim and very bad news for John.

As a young woman and brand-new detective, Julia admits that it has been hard at times to get people to take her seriously, especially on things like stalking or a suspicious missing person case. There are so many cases that detectives have to work on, it can be challenging to find time to work on a case like what had been reported about John. When there is a serial rapist or unsolved murder demanding the attention of the department, detectives may feel like they don't have any choice but to tell victims of seemingly less menacing offenders like an aggressive ex to block his number and hope he'll go away. Detective Bowman said that, as they saw with John, oftentimes these seemingly small crimes are a direct link to an incredibly dangerous person who will continue to escalate over time.

When Detective Bowman took over the case, she reinterviewed the victim and learned that she and John had met at the hospital. She had been a patient recovering from brain surgery. John identified himself as her anesthesiologist, gave her a card with his phone number, and offered to help her in any way that she needed. Focused on her recovery and having all of the support she needed at the hospital, she didn't reach out to him. But the two crossed paths in the hospital a few weeks later, recognized each other, and started a conversation. To this day we have no idea why or how he was working in that hospital.

The two acknowledged that meeting in a hospital where she was a patient and he worked on her case was not ideal and agreed to reconnect on the dating website Plenty of Fish, where they both happened to have a membership.

Detective Bowman asked the victim to share the correspondence the two had on the site and then eventually over email. It took some time to compile and organize all of the communications—more than 1,300 messages to comb through and no tools like we have today to speed up the process by summarizing the content or pulling keywords.

Reading the messages, it was very clear that John was skilled at making her feel very special, needed, and appreciated. Bowman could see how John asked pointed questions that highlighted what she was most insecure about and afraid of. He learned what had failed in her previous relationships and used that information to create a relationship that felt like exactly what she needed.

Shortly after they started dating, the two agreed that it didn't make sense for her to live in her ex-husband's house, so she rented a place in Laguna Beach for them. He isolated her from friends, from her children, and from her ex-husband, who was her friend and business partner.

And for a short time, she was very taken by the persona that John had created. He posed as a busy anesthesiologist. Whenever she saw him, it seemed he was in scrubs and always on his way to or from hospitals. He explained that he was an independent contractor as an anesthesiologist, hired by surgeons for their surgeries as needed. As a result, his schedule was erratic. Sometimes he was available and sometimes he wasn't.

John began talking to her about her financial situation. He positioned himself to be the hero who would save her from her ex-husband. She was also having financial issues—she had considerable amounts of money, all located out of the country, but she was unable to access it without paying significant penalties. He managed to persuade her that if she wired him all of her money, she wouldn't have to pay the penalties she was concerned about. He convinced her that he was good with finances and that he could look at all of her documents.

She gave him access to millions of dollars, titles, and deeds to houses. She shared all of her financial information—the trust for her children, all of her banking information—thinking he would help her. He had access to all of her accounts and then convinced her to initiate a wire transfer of all of her money to his accounts, where her funds would be safer.

Thankfully, because she was transferring millions of dollars internationally, the process took thirty days. About fifteen days into the transfer process, she started to get cold feet about moving so much money without telling anyone else. So she told a friend about John.

The friend did an internet search for John and first found a "John Meehan" living in Laguna Niguel who was a doctor. They started calling hospitals, asking if there was a John Meehan working there as an anesthesiologist. No one had ever heard of him.

The friend did a deeper dive on the internet and found websites where women talk about their horrible ex-boyfriends, and John Meehan was all over the sites.

> *This man is a fraud. He claims to be an anesthesiologist or a nurse anesthetist. He is neither... check with the state boards in California. He is a convicted felon, check with the OTIS site in Michigan Department of Corrections. He conned me out of money and will nickel and dime you to death before he is done with you.*
>
> *He is very good looking. He has two children with their mother back east with whom he is in constant legal battle. He will travel far to come meet you. He has a sarcastic manner and knows every trick in the book to make you fall for him. Trust your intuition ladies. He is a pathologically rotten apple!*
>
> *I have a medical background and I checked him out. Drug addict is what he is...been to prison too. State of TN Nursing board says he was stealing drugs from ER and has no license at all. Same in California. Good storyteller: always it is the women who were bad to him.*
>
> *He is an equal opportunity player—male and female.*

> *Well, here I am, his latest victim. I met John on match and found all of the above to be absolutely true.*
>
> *He drives an 8-10-year-old White Ford Explorer with white paint splashed all over the back bumper...kind of dinged and dented. ...dress shirts and jeans. Now he sports an exposed tendon coming out of his right foot. He said he tripped and fell on a wire on the pool heater. I think he had a massive infection from shooting up in the vein. He clearly has oodles of drugs.*
>
> *OMG! I have been talking and texting with this man I know now to be a creep. I felt like things were not adding up and I started to question him. I found him on plenty of fish going under the name Bboles0897 saying "bet I can make you laugh" So fast forward to this point. Everything that has been written above is true. He has said all those things to me and he is a bad man. Stay away!*

John's new girlfriend confronted him about what was on the websites, and he was furious. He then started to notice that the wire transfer wasn't moving along and got even angrier. She had found out who he really was in time to stop the money transfer.

The love-bombing abruptly stopped. John switched to intimidation, showing her a gun and a backpack filled with cash. He told her how powerful he was and what he was capable of, hoping she would give in and pay him to go away. She did realize that she needed to leave him, but their lives were so intertwined at that point, and he had so much access to her and her personal information.

Since she had stopped the wire transfer, John couldn't access her money, but neither could she. He had all of her cash because he'd said it was safer with him, so she couldn't provide for herself in even the most basic ways.

After she managed to separate from him, John broke into her house and left a page from her passport with a note that said, "We need to talk." So now she knew that he had found and stolen her passport. She went to visit a friend in a gated community in Newport Beach, and John got a visitor pass to that private community, wrote a threat on the pass, and left it inside her car. So now she knew he had a key to her car. She would be driving and suddenly see John in his car right behind her, pointing at her as soon as she noticed him. She started sleeping in her ex-husband's office and woke up one morning to find John standing outside the glass door of the building. She kept telling him to leave her alone, but that just seemed to make him angrier.

Like so many of John's victims, a lot of what kept her from reaching out for help was shame. So many women who find themselves the victim of a stalker think they've done this to themselves by not doing enough research on a guy before getting into a relationship with them. After all, she gave him access to her finances. She separated herself from friends and family. For too long, she suffered in silence, just hoping he'd grow tired of hunting her and go away, too embarrassed to ask for help.

Her hopelessness probably greatly increased when, after finally mustering up enough courage to ask the police for help, she discovered that even they couldn't keep John from harassing her. I would imagine she thought, *He's just calling me, and you can call people. He's sometimes in the same place that I am. That's not a crime.* But it is. It is a crime to call someone over and over and over again. It is a crime to email someone incessantly. And once you've told them explicitly to stop and they choose to continue, they're committing a crime. It's a misdemeanor in most cases, but it's a start.

When I talked to Julia about this case that started more than ten years ago, she shared some of what she was learning then and how it applies to stalking cases today.

"The problem with stalking is that the stalkers will start with things like calling you incessantly or emailing you incessantly. It's volatile because you don't know how it's going to escalate," she explained. "But as law enforcement, we know it will escalate. It could become violent. It could be more just brazen invasions of your property, or your space, or your privacy, or whatever, but we know it will escalate."

For John's victim in 2014, it went from emails and text messages to breaking into her house, to breaking into her car, to leaving her these notes, to stealing her passport, which, again, is emotional terrorism. He convinced her that she couldn't leave.

The challenge with someone like John is that he knew everybody else's stuff. He meticulously gathered information and, when he needed it, used it against all of his victims. He was careful to never leave a trace—he didn't have a cell phone in his name, a car registered to him, or a California driver's license. In 2014, he didn't have any mail going to any address that we were aware of, so it made it difficult for anyone to find him.

Once Detective Bowman was on the case, the first thing she tried was a ruse where she used the victim's phone to text John. She said she'd give John all the money he believed he was owed.

She tried to set up a meeting at a coffee shop, but he didn't take the bait.

Officers arrived early, conducted counter-surveillance, and were confident they weren't made, but he never showed. Hours later, he sent her an email saying, "I know you've called law enforcement. I know that they were waiting for me."

Undeterred, the sergeant working with Bowman had a very creative idea for how they might find him. The victim had told us that she'd seen a lot of orange pill bottles that were prescribed to him. She was sure he had an opioid addiction and that he needed a lot of pills to support his habit. He also talked about all kinds of injuries he had that required prescriptions. In 2014, there was a database where law enforcement could run anyone's name and birthday to find out every medication they'd ever been prescribed, the name of the prescribing physician, and where they had that prescription filled. Today, that same search requires a warrant, but at the time, they didn't need one.

The team had a narcotics detective run that report on John and found that he had a chiropractor in Cathedral City that he saw regularly. Law enforcement contacted the chiropractor and asked him to reach out to John and schedule an appointment. The chiropractor readily agreed.

After nearly four months of trying to find John and recognizing that his behavior was escalating, they finally had a way of knowing exactly where he would be and when.

On July 1, Detective Bowman, her detective sergeant, and a narcotics detective drove out to wait for John to arrive for his chiropractic appointment. It was over a hundred degrees out, and they waited in their car in the parking lot because they didn't know what kind of car John was driving. Around two, the time of his appointment, a red Jeep pulled into the lot and out walked John. Julia remembers thinking it was like seeing a movie star without their makeup on or something—he did not look like the pictures. He was wearing ratty old basketball shorts and a wrinkled T-shirt. He was not clean-shaven. He just looked disheveled.

John's mugshots.

Detective Bowman approached John in the waiting room and introduced herself as a detective with the Laguna Beach Police Department. She asked if, to respect his privacy, they could go outside. John was completely calm and agreed to go outside with her and the other officers.

Once they were outside, Detective Bowman explained to John that he wasn't under arrest, but that he wasn't free to leave either. Since it was July, she was also able to add, "It's really hot outside. That doesn't bother me, but if you would be more comfortable, my air-conditioned detective car is right over there. We can go sit in my car."

John agreed to sit in her car, and Bowman had the sense that this was playing out perfectly in John's mind. He felt like he was controlling the situation. He chose where they were going to go.

All three of them went with John to their car, Julia sitting in the front seat with John, and the other detective and detective sergeant in the back seat. Julia told John, "You can leave the door open if you want. We're not trying to box you in here," which was a smart move because she hadn't Mirandized him. She reminded him he wasn't free to leave, but he also wasn't under arrest. She wanted to cover all her bases and worried that if she closed the door, he would be able to say he felt like he was in custody.

Julia's reflections a decade later about her interview with John that day were fascinating. She acknowledges that she was a young detective, but anyone listening to her talk can tell that she understands the criminal mind. Thinking about that day, she shared, "I found with guys in sex assault and domestic violence relationships, when I interview them, they see me as a challenge to conquer. I think in John's case, when he kind of sized me up and realized I wasn't going to fall for his bullshit, I wasn't someone who he could swoon with his charisma, then it became this challenge of he's going to beat me in a match of wits or something, which is great because what that does for me is it just keeps him talking. And the more he talks, the more lies that come out. I'd done months of investigation. I was very clear on what the timeline was, what the crimes were, what the evidence was behind each of those crimes."

Detective Bowman realized that John was obviously very intelligent, or he was at least very good at managing complicated lies. Her goal didn't change: She needed him to agree to a list of statements related to stalking his ex-girlfriend so that he couldn't deny his connection to the incidents at a later date.

The longer they talked, the angrier John got at Julia, even though she remained calm and never raised her voice. The two male detectives in the back of the car occasionally called John out on a lie he had told, but he never got upset with them. He'd be visibly agitated by what they were saying but then turn all of his anger toward Julia.

Eventually, things had gone on too long, and John said he was done. When he got out of the car, the officer in the back got out as well and stopped him, letting John know that he was officially under arrest.

Julia remembered something important that day that people reading about or listening to John's story may not realize. John was a big guy.

"When they were standing next to each other, the arresting officer is six feet tall, 230 pounds. John was bigger than him. He was a big guy, a big barrel-chested guy. And he looked very weathered, and obviously he had a substance abuse [problem], but he was a big guy."

John could and would have been very intimidating, even if he had a smaller stature, but his size made everything he said and did that much more terrifying. Julia went on to say, "I was thinking this would be so physically intimidating if this was the man that's coming to your front door, or in the car behind you, or threatening you. He's a large man, and he clearly has a very fiery temper. And if I'd been alone, I would not have felt comfortable sitting in the car with him or putting hands on him, which is why I bring my bouncers."

It was a good reminder from Julia that, when dealing with people like John, there's no shame in asking for help. Know what you're up against and go in prepared.

Except for asking what he was being charged with, John didn't say anything for the two-hour ride back to Laguna Beach. They got a search warrant for his Jeep. After going through

John's car, they learned that the car was registered to one of his ex-girlfriends. She had tried to file a report with the police previously because he had extorted her for the very car they were searching.

In the Jeep, they found John's mail, with an address of an RV park in Cathedral City. They obtained a search warrant for John's RV and, still in the blazing heat, went to check it out. Unsure of the best way to access the RV, one of the officers tried the door, and John had left it unlocked. They walked right in and executed their search.

The RV was filthy, with boxes of food and clothes scattered throughout. There seemed to be insects on every surface and a thick fog in the air. Detective Bowman said it looked like the inspiration for *Breaking Bad*—needles and pills throughout the RV.

But the Laguna Beach detectives weren't looking at John for a drug charge. What stood out to them was the one thing in John's home that wasn't filthy: a desktop computer and monitor. It was pristine. The mouse was in front of it on the little kitchen table in the RV, and when Julia shook the mouse, the monitor turned on. It wasn't password-protected and, when the monitor woke up, the entire screen was filled with JPG images of women. And several of them, even though they were each the size of a dime, were recognizable as John's victims they had met researching John's case. Detective Bowman even saw her victim on the screen.

John's online dating profile pic, posing with Abby as a perfect dad.

To search the computer, they needed another search warrant, so they seized the computer, but they couldn't look through it right away. They also collected the scrubs John so famously wore and their victim's passport that he had stolen.

But that was just the beginning. Detective Bowman had found a thread, and she kept pulling, unraveling more and more of John's carefully crafted life.

Detectives found another car registered to John and, more importantly, more mail that linked him to an office building a couple of blocks away. They obtained another search warrant for the new location and then went to the office building. When they opened the door, they found a couch, a motorcycle, and a refrigerator, and then just piles and piles of paperwork everywhere.

Detective Bowman knew from her stalking courses that men like John are often hoarders. They often keep the very evidence that will lead to their downfall, and John was no exception, though it wasn't immediately apparent.

As they walked farther into the building, they found a boat, tools, and a bunch of junk. There was nothing obviously criminal, and Detective Bowman started to worry that this had been a wild goose chase. But her reputation was on the line, so she wasn't about to give up.

They eventually uncovered paperwork that was evidence of stalking behavior: photocopies of Facebook pages, dating profiles, and pages that were just handwritten lists of social security numbers, pictures of driver's licenses, social security cards, passports, and financial documents. None of them belonged to John Meehan.

There were also letters, mortgage statements, and utility bills for me, his sister, and a long list of other women. He never lost interest in any of them. Even if he found a new victim, his previous victims never left his mind.

Curiously, they also found the entire police report for his brother's overdose. They had talked to Dennis Luken, and they did know about his drug arrest in Ohio, so it was easy to guess why John would have been interested in the details of that report.

But the biggest find was yet to come. When detectives looked in the refrigerator, they discovered it was empty. But when they looked in the freezer, they found a black backpack. When they opened it, they found a revolver, hundreds of rounds of ammo, cyanide capsules and powder, duct tape, zip ties, Garmin GPS units, and binoculars. When they laid it out, it became obvious that it was a kidnapping or killing kit. As a felon, John was prohibited from possessing a firearm or having the ammo, which resulted in additional charges. But the rest of the contents validated the suspicions they had. If they had not arrested John that day, he was going to kidnap and kill someone, and Julia was right to follow her suspicions.

John was already in county jail when they added charges to his arrest. I was reminded that, whether John's family ties to the mafia were exaggerated or not, he definitely embraced the motto of the organized crime families he saw in the movies: Don't get mad, get even. His response to his arrest was, while he was in custody, to try to put a hit out on me, Detective Bowman, and the female officer who initially took the case. He didn't go after any of the men involved in his arrest—not his chiropractor, the detective sergeant, or the other male detective present at his arrest.

Continuing with his same tricks, when Detective Bowman went to serve John with an additional restraining order, she learned that he had been transferred to the medical ward. John had cut his femoral artery, and the jail personnel deemed the act a suicide attempt until Detective Bowman shared his detailed history with them. Not only did he have the medical expertise to kill himself if he really wanted to, but he had also pulled similar stunts to get drugs and even attempted to escape.

All of this hard work came to a somewhat unsatisfying end. John was offered and accepted a plea deal because his victim for this case had left the country and wasn't willing to return for a trial. Without her testimony, the district attorney didn't feel they could get more than two years, so that's what he served.

Detective Bowman and the female officer who originally spoke to John tried to get a restraining order against him based on the fact that John had tried to have them killed. The DA said no because they were police officers and it was part of the job. He didn't believe they should feel threatened or intimidated by John. But he didn't know what it was like to be in John's sights. His hatred of women and commitment to revenge were terrifying, and they had every right to be afraid.

A few years later, Detective Bowman learned the fate of John Meehan when a friend called to tell her what had happened. But it wasn't until she listened to the *Dirty John* podcast that she learned that John met his next victim just two days after he was released from prison.

CHAPTER 17

THANK GOD IT IS OVER

John was killed.

—EMAIL SUBJECT LINE FROM KAREN, JOHN'S SISTER

On August 24, 2016, at the age of fifty-seven, John Michael Meehan died. If you're reading this book, you have probably heard the podcast, watched some version of the story on TV, or read about it online. But in case you missed it, here's a short version of the end of John's life.

On October 10, 2014, just two days after being released from prison for violating a restraining order, John met a woman named Debra Newell. John gained Debra's trust in the same way he connected with the other women he manipulated. He lied about who he was, identified and exploited everything that was most important to her, and then attempted to separate her from her family and gain access to her money. In December of 2014, John convinced Debra to marry him, but it wasn't long before she had serious doubts about him and attempted to leave their relationship.

Their time together is Debra's story to tell, which she did—in a podcast, a book, and a variety of different interviews. Like me, Debra is committed to sharing her story to help others avoid predators like John. But there's one additional piece of the story that we have to include here, before sharing how John's death impacted my family.

In March of 2016, Debra separated from John for what would be the last time in a series of breakups and make-ups—something that most of us have experienced at some point in our lives and, as I would come to learn, is common in domestic abuse situations. But she finally accepted that John was a con artist, not worth the love and forgiveness she had been willing to offer. John seemed to sense that this was a real end to their relationship and resorted to violent acts none of us had seen before.

In an attempt to stay safe during separation, Debra had gone into hiding, changing her appearance and moving out of her house. When John couldn't find her, he did what we know his mafia mentality deemed appropriate. He went for her family. On August 20, 2016, John parked his car at the apartment building where Terra Newell, Debra's daughter, who was twenty-five at the time, lived. He waited for her to return home from work. Police would later find what they called a "kidnap kit" in his car—duct tape, cable ties, and kitchen knives.

When Terra arrived home from work, John approached her from behind and attacked her. The two fought and, despite John's significant body size advantage, Terra managed to kick the knife out of John's hand and grab it herself. Though she was injured, Terra stabbed John thirteen times, including once through his left eye.

A resident of the apartment complex heard the fight and called the police, who arrived with paramedics. They treated Terra and John at the scene and then transported both separately to the hospital. Terra was treated and released. John was declared brain dead and kept on life support so that his immediate family could be notified of what had happened.

A clear case of self-defense, no charges were filed against Terra.

The day life support was to be pulled, I was at work. It was an otherwise normal Wednesday until I received an email from John's sister Karen.

> *Subject: John was killed*
>
> *Call me*
>
> *Karen XXXXXXXXXX*
>
> *He had very little belongings. Does your daughters want his diplomas? If not we will throw them out. The is no funeral*

I think I started trembling, though I'm not sure if my shaking was visible on the outside. I remember that inside it felt like a seven on the Richter scale. In shock, I burst into tears when I saw my friend Natalie, who was also a nurse. I didn't know any of the details of how John had died yet, but all of the emotions, terror, and hurt from the past decades defending myself against John all came pouring out.

Karen's email had said to call her, but she had typed her phone number incorrectly, and I didn't have a way to reach her immediately. I called Donna instead, and she filled me in on all the details.

I had popped into one of the gastroenterologists' offices and was frantically taking notes. I couldn't believe my ears. *Attacked his ex-wife's daughter. Stabbed in the eye.* I had predicted that John would go down in a ball of fire, but this scenario never crossed my mind. I immediately wondered how I would break this to Emily and Abby.

It was near the end of the day, and I asked the other nurse anesthetist to finish the last case I had been assigned. I was in no shape to keep working with patients. Augie was also at work, and although I didn't want to tell him as I knew it would consume his thoughts when he needed to be focused on his patients, I felt I had to call him before anyone else. As anesthetists, it's important to be focused and not distracted, but sometimes it can't be helped.

Augie didn't answer my call, which told me he was busy taking care of a patient. When I drove home, I stopped at my sister's house. We lived in the same neighborhood, and I practically passed her house going to mine. So that day, I sat her down at her kitchen table and told her what had happened. We cried together, but not really because John had died. We cried with relief that this was finally over.

I knew the very next person who deserved to know about John's death was Denny Luken. He answered my call right away, and I said, "Denny, this is the call you have been waiting for." I knew that Denny would be glad to hear that John had finally gotten exactly what he deserved.

As I had conversations with people who had known John, I was also considering another tricky fact. Technically, John was only brain-dead, which meant he would never regain consciousness and could not survive without the machines that were currently breathing for him, but his next of kin would be asked to make decisions for his medical care. Since John had been attacking Debra's daughter when he was fatally injured, I was told that Debra didn't feel she should make the decision about his life support. Karen and I agreed that it wasn't appropriate to even consider asking my daughters, sixteen and twenty-one years old, so Karen made the decision to discontinue his life support.

When John died, Emily had just been accepted into nursing school. She was so happy. And we were so proud of her. Nursing school is so competitive, and it had been a rough road for her to get to where she was in August of 2016. She had moved to Augusta and was settled into her new home, eagerly awaiting her white coat ceremony to be held on August 26.

Abby was doing well in high school, playing lacrosse, and spending time with friends—just a typical, happy teenager. Both girls were thriving and living their best lives.

Augie and I were working as nurse anesthetists and had recently purchased a vacation home on Lake Rabun. After so many years of hard work, we were finally enjoying the fruits of our labor. We spent most weekends relaxing, boating, and entertaining. I loved having the girls invite their friends to the lake house where I would just enjoy cooking for them and watching them spend time with each other. It was like we were living in a dream.

I wanted to tell the girls what had happened in person, and since Emily's white coat ceremony was on the 26th, just two days after John had been declared brain-dead and taken off life support, we'd all be together then. Augie, Abby, and I drove to Augusta together and celebrated Emily on the 26th, staying in town for one more night.

The next morning, I told Augie that I felt that I should tell the girls by myself, just the three of us. He drove me to a fast-food restaurant where I picked up breakfast for the girls, and then he dropped me off at Emily's apartment, where Abby had spent the night.

We made small talk, and the girls finished their breakfast. They went and sat on the couch, and I pulled up a dining room chair so that I could sit in front of both of them.

I knew that whatever I said in this moment would never be forgotten, so I tried to choose my words wisely. I started by saying that I had something important to tell them.

"You remember that your dad got married, right?" I was trying to find a way to ease into a conversation about their largely absent father. I thought it must have felt to them like it was coming out of the blue.

I told them about how John had attacked Terra, that she had fought back, and that John had lost the battle.

Working in the medical field, I have learned that there is no single way that people respond to traumatic information, so I tried to be prepared for anything. Emily let out a sigh and a little laugh. She said, "I thought you were going to tell us that Nana had died or something."

Abby had a different reaction. I looked at her and saw she was crying. And then she got mad at Emily for laughing. As expected, we went through a wide range of emotions. But we worked through our feelings about John's death together, as a family. Our weekend would end abruptly as Abby, Augie, and I traveled back home, leaving Emily alone in a town where she essentially knew no one. Each of the girls would continue to have their own reactions to the news. Emily's would come by way of a panic attack in class while discussing organ donation in a nursing class. Abby would share that she was having thoughts of her dead father being able to see her now. Emily was able to work through this outburst of emotion with some help from me, and Abby's concerns were squashed by Augie, who told her that only people in heaven are given that privilege.

In the days and weeks that followed, I told more and more people what had happened. I called my friend Jane, who had reported John to the Indiana Board of Nursing and had been afraid he would retaliate in some way. I heard the relief she felt in her response to the news. I left a message for John's ex-fiancée in Michigan. When she called me back, she had already guessed why I was calling. I also notified my dear neighbors in Ohio, the Schikners, who were instrumental in supporting me during my divorce from John. I told the story of his last day over and over again. He had hurt so many people, and it was finally sinking in that he was gone. His reign of terror had ended.

In 2016, it had been more than a decade since I had last seen John. The last time I physically laid eyes on him was around 2005, when we were battling out post-prison visitation. After that, he had three supervised visitations that Augie took the girls to, and then none of us ever saw him again.

There was no memorial for John. For a split second I thought it would help to attend a service so that I could see firsthand that John was dead. Karen had taken pictures and sent them to Donna, and I realized immediately that I didn't want anything to do with that. But it wasn't long before my phone was pinging with photos of John in a cardboard box and a video of his cremation. I asked Augie to look at the pictures first. Eventually I did look at the pictures, and they were horrifying. The natural decay that had occurred since he had died and the injury to his eye made him practically unrecognizable.

Karen explained that she had placed two necklaces on his chest and had taken a lock of his hair. She asked if I wanted any of his burial items or his ashes for the girls. I quickly and confidently said no. I didn't want anything of his anywhere near my house. It all felt evil to me.

I did, however, give something to Karen for John's cremation. A few days after his death, I wrote him a letter. I kept having conversations with John in my head. Some of what I was thinking was very angry, and I realized I still had questions: *Who in the hell are you? What the hell have you done?*

Now that I knew I wouldn't ever have the opportunity to say these things to John for closure, I wanted to get them out on paper. So I sat at my desk and wrote the letter, emailed it to Karen, and asked her to print and deliver it to his dead body before cremation. It was a cathartic experience. All I needed was to send these words to John.

> *Since I will never have the opportunity to say these things in person, I need to let you know the following:*
>
> *Your children are beautiful, kind, strong, and love God. I have spent years piecing together their broken hearts caused by your choices. They are survivors and will have fulfilling and blessed lives despite the great loss many years ago of the man who was supposed to love them the most. I cannot even pretend to understand that kind of disappointment or pain.*
>
> *You have spent most of your adult life taking advantage of and torturing everyone in your path.*

You were calculated and took joy in the game of recreating yourself over and over again. You were clearly a tortured soul who we may never fully understand, but I cannot be convinced that you didn't know right from wrong. You consistently chose "wrong" and chose yourself over all else. Lives have forever been altered, but you need to know that you destroyed no one but yourself.

I do not have a single good thought about you and I am looking forward to my future as I slowly forget all of the torment to my family, your family and countless women who were all fooled by you. We are ALL going to live long abundant lives despite your harsh words and countless threats.

I have absolutely no hate in my heart for you and I forgive you so that I may heal and be a healing force for the two beautiful girls I have raised.

Goodbye. Thank God it is over.

CHAPTER 18

THE FIRST WIFE

No more lies because the truth will never die.

—THEME SONG FROM THE FIRST WIFE PODCAST

When I learned that John had died attacking a young woman, I assumed it would make the news. I didn't know it would become a wildly popular podcast and Netflix series, but I knew in the days that followed his death, I'd be able to look online and find an article in a local paper about it. On the day I learned John died and over the following weeks, I checked local papers and found more information about what had happened and what had been shared with the public.

About a month after John's death, on September 16, I received an email from Hannah Fry, a Newport Beach reporter writing for the *Daily Putilot.* I didn't really know it at the time, but I was in good hands. Hannah would go on to become a staff writer for the *LA Times* and she was very easy to work with, especially considering how anxious I was from the start about sharing anything about John.

Hannah requested an interview, which I initially declined. I was a bit exhausted and overwhelmed and didn't really have it in me to talk to a total stranger for hours. I eventually followed up and requested she send a list of questions. I came to see value in sharing what I knew about John's life. Reading my answers to her questions nearly ten years later reminds me how little I really knew about John before he died. So much information was to come in the following months and years.

The following is my email response with her questions included for clarity.

> *Hannah,*
>
> *I have reservations about participating but am hoping that you will respect me and my daughters in the process. We have traveled a long and painful road so I hope that you appreciate that and will put our personal experience and pain above an article that will be very interesting but soon forgotten by most.*
>
> ***How much do your daughters know about John and what has been their reaction?***
>
> *I cannot speak for my girls but I can tell you that I believe the life he led was more painful than his death. They know most of the details. Some unnecessary and sensitive details have been omitted.*

How often did John contact you and your daughters and what was the context of those conversations/visits?

They have not had contact with John since 2005. He was awarded supervised visitation I believe in 2004 and only saw them 3 times during the year following.

What do you think John's motivation was for the way he lived his life? (Context for this question: it seems as though he had a drug problem. Do you think he met and manipulated women to fund his lifestyle and purchase drugs or was it something else?)

I do not think JMM needed women to fund his drug problem. He definitely preyed on wealthy, beautiful and seemingly intelligent women. Of the women I have been in contact with over the years it seems our intelligence was limited to the mind and not the heart. JMM seemed to have a desire to be a big shot based on the lies of telling women he was an attorney or an anesthesiologist. He indeed completed training for and was a practicing CRNA but the prestige that came with this level of advanced practice nursing was not enough for him. I believe he was a sociopath. Striking similarity to the guy chronicled in the "Catch Me If You Can" movie. His needs were first and it didn't matter who he stomped on in the process of getting those needs met. I never knew him to have a drug problem while we were together. That doesn't mean he didn't.

What was your family's reaction when you learned that John had died?

I was not shocked that John died. I have been anticipating it for years. I was actually quite relieved that the pain and torment to so many of us was over, and that there would be no new victims. I imagined it would be a drug overdose or gun shot from an angry male relative of someone he took advantage of. I was saddened by the fact that I had to explain it to my children.

I've read in court papers that you were the one who alerted police to John stealing drugs from the hospital where you both worked while you were married. Is that true, and if so, what led you to make that decision? If not, what happened?

We were already separating at the time I found the drugs and I was informed by a family member that he was mailing narcotics to his brother in California. I felt an ethical obligation as a medical professional to report it. I also feared for the safety of my children being with someone who was impaired.

I've read that you and John met in college. Can you please describe the circumstances

surrounding your first meeting with John and your first impression?

I was not that interested really after our first meeting, but John soon becomes exactly what you are looking for. In hindsight I feel it was very calculated. I married a man with a birth certificate that said 1964 but discovered that he was born in 1959 in 2000 after our separation.

At what point in your relationship did John's behavior begin to change and what were the changes? Was John ever abusive (physically, emotionally, ect.) to you or your daughters and how did that typically manifest? How did John react when you filed for divorce?

I felt a distancing from him not knowing that he had initiated a relationship with a medical resident in another state. He filed for divorce not me. This gave me the courage to look into and discover new details and really address some red flags that I had either dismissed or JMM had lied his way out of. John was never verbally or physically abusive. That would have been counterproductive in his manipulative scheme.

Did you ever suspect that John would attempt to kill anyone? Why or why not?

Post 2000, as his life and career were spiraling, JMM threatened anyone who got in his way, but I never knew him to be violent with anyone. I

> *would say that I knew to be terrified of him. Just a sense that I had. He was a cyber terrorist for sure. He harassed and sued anyone and everyone. He was very caustic, crude and litigious when shielded by his computer screen. In reality he seemed a coward. I did become very concerned when they found zip ties, guns, cyanide, etc. during a search warrant in 2014.*
>
> *I would be interested and willing to check your article for accuracy. I know this story better than anyone and since I have now participated would want it told correctly.*

Hannah's reply to my answers was sincere, and it made me feel even more confident that sharing what I knew was the right thing to do.

> *Thank you very much for taking the time to answer these questions. I understand your hesitation and your need to protect your daughters. My hope is that the women who were hurt by John will find some relief. I believe there are at least a few women (if not many) out there who might not know what happened to him and may still be living in fear.*

My interactions with Hannah and then Chris Goffard, who would eventually bring national attention to the case by reporting and hosting the *Dirty John* podcast created by Wondery and the *Los Angeles Times,* were very positive. Other reporters reached out as well, but those interactions are all a blur. When people ask what reporters successfully connected with me and my family, I usually tell them that the people who did their research and understood who they were talking to had the best luck. Hannah and Chris, as well as others, were informed and respectful, and it made it much easier for me to engage with them.

Initially Chris had proposed a series of detailed articles in the *LA Times*, and I agreed to help him in any way that I could. From the start, I sensed that he would tell the story well and be careful to report the facts. He was so informed that his investigation and eventual podcast revealed things about John that I didn't know, most notably that he had tried to put a hit out on me while he was in prison. It had happened a few years earlier, and nothing came of the attempt, but it was still a terrifying thought. And I had no idea until Chris told me about it.

Eventually, Chris told me that he was thinking John's story would make a great podcast. In 2016, I didn't even know what that meant. Even though they're part of our everyday lives now, they weren't really that popular until 2014, and even in 2016, I was barely aware of them. But I trusted Chris, so I was onboard.

When Wondery launched *Dirty John* in 2017, they released an episode a week, and I was eager to listen to every episode. What I didn't fully realize at the time was that I was one of five million people listening.

I had no idea what to expect. Since I wasn't familiar with podcasts, I definitely didn't realize how professional the production would be. Chris narrated the podcast, and interview clips from his research were woven together with music that perfectly matched the tone of the story. And Tracy Bonham's song "Devil's Got Your Boyfriend" was perfect. I loved it.

Matt Murphy, whom I would come to know better over the next few years, opened the podcast with a shocking discussion of John's injuries. "There are a total of thirteen stab wounds..." was a startling opening line to hear, even though I already knew the information being shared. There was something about hearing it, in the context of this podcast, from someone reporting on John's death, that made it feel a bit surreal. I was hooked from the start.

As I talked to more people about my life with John, I also started learning more about the people working in the media who were helping the victims of people like John. Early on, I listened to *Real Crime Profile* and knew I wanted to meet Laura Richards. I was fascinated by how she spoke about John and the language she used to explain him without ever having met him. I remember thinking, *This woman gets it.* I ended up meeting Laura on one of my trips to LA. We had lunch with Debra Newell and her daughter Jacqueline, and I enjoyed getting to know all of them a little more.

At the *Dirty John* limited series premiere event, Laura Richards introduced me to Aliza Rosen, a media professional, and both were initially interested in collaborating on a potential book deal. I was immediately intrigued by the idea because I had already talked to a ghostwriter about a book that had just never taken off. But it seems I wasn't destined to write a book at that time, as the idea soon changed into a podcast proposal.

It was pretty incredible to go from barely knowing what a podcast was to helping Aliza pitch a podcast about my life with John. Laura Richards would also be an executive producer, and from the start, I knew these women knew what they were doing and that I could trust them, both as experts navigating this new project and as people who would take great care when helping me tell my story.

Audible picked up our podcast, and we were off and running. I was an executive producer, though I again found myself not entirely sure of what that meant. I ended up working closely with Aliza, Laura, and Leah Rothman, our writer, and was able to share a lot of input as they wrote the content for the podcast. I was especially appreciative of the fact that our team of creators was all female. We definitely had great technical support from a few different men and, of course, several key interviews were with men, but the design and delivery being driven by a team of women really contributed to delivering the right message—that John was a predator.

I provided contacts and helped shape the storyline of the podcast, but Leah contacted and interviewed all of the participants. When I listened to their interviews, helping to put the content together, I found myself learning more about John—things that I had never expected.

One of the most surprising interviews was with Mark, one of John's friends. I had known Mark as he was a student in John's anesthesia training in Tennessee and I knew him to be one of the people who John was close to in his class. There were huge revelations when I finally reached out to Mark for my Audible podcast.

Mark very candidly shared his experience with John, frequently questioning his behavior, even though he never really confronted John about his choices. Mark recounted how he had walked in on John having sex in a call room with one of their married instructors and again at Mark's apartment with classmates who had all crashed at his place after a study session. He also shared that John repeatedly invited him to go to Vegas.

John showed him tapes of John having sex with what Mark described as drug-addicted, unhealthy women. Mark didn't want any part of it, but John kept asking.

I was not surprised to hear from Mark that John had been flirtatious with him, even though I hadn't heard any stories of John having sexual relationships with men. I suspected that their relationship may have been more than just friends after reading their email correspondence when I was looking through John's hard drive for evidence that John had affairs and that he had sent drugs to his brother. Emails where John joked with Mark about "a blow job he owed him" made it seem like they had more than a platonic friendship. But Mark said that he was never attracted to John, and that, even though there were some innuendos from John, they never had a physical relationship.

The other shocking and most personally disturbing thing I heard from Mark was that John wanted to "punish and slay as many women as possible." It was such a strange thing to say. It made me think that all of his affairs weren't just about sex. I had to consider that it even meant that how he treated me and the other women he was in relationships with wasn't about not caring. He seemed to have truly wanted to harm us.

A true psychopath, John never thought about the future, so the consequences Mark was warning him about simply didn't register with him. But John did realize that if he could pass a disease on to a woman, leave her wondering if her husband was the father of an unplanned baby or if it was John, or abandon a single woman to terminate a pregnancy or raise a child alone, he could successfully disrupt her life forever. The thought of any of those results undoubtedly brought him immense joy because, no matter the outcome, they would be tremendously stressful for the woman he had been with.

Other than Mark's interview, there were also individual stories that hit harder than others. It was a little strange because, at the time I was hearing all of these details about how terribly John lived his life, I was happily married to Augie. I had a good understanding that John hadn't ever really cared about me, but some things still hurt to hear. One of those stories was when I learned the details of where John was on my thirtieth birthday.

John and I always celebrated on our own timeline. It's something a lot of people who work in the medical field do, because we are often working on holidays or at odd times of the day. It's just part of the job. So when he was in California visiting friends and family over my thirtieth birthday, while I was pregnant with our first child, I didn't even really think that much of it. But hearing from Kathy, his former coworker from the law firm where he was a clerk, that he had actually gone to California to see her was surprisingly hurtful. The feeling passed fairly quickly, but I was still surprised that I could feel that kind of hurt when I didn't have any feelings of love for John at all.

Of course, reconnecting with people was also filled with really positive experiences. I had the chance to reconnect with my attorney, Ellen, and we caught up with each other like old friends. She was my safe space during some of my most difficult times with John. Ellen helped me navigate complicated legal issues that were made even more difficult to endure because of the mental and emotional stress of the situation. Talking to her always reminds me just how critical she was not just to my success in court but to my survival of those years.

Detective Denny Luken, always eager to know how the girls and I are doing, was quick to respond when I reached out. I've never lost touch with him, but of course, since John's death, we just haven't spoken as often. I enjoyed catching up with him and hearing about his family. Each time we talk I'm reminded that he is a fierce protector of those who need him. It is in his very nature and, even in his retirement, I can see the passion he still carries for justice.

Bringing my support network together for the podcast was wonderful, and an important reminder that, even if it takes a few tries to find them, there are people working in the legal system who can and will help the people who need it. I am always grateful and amazed at how people still step up for me all these years later. John ruined so many people, and we all still need each other from time to time to continue our healing. Hearing from the people who truly were my lifelines during those dark times was incredible.

Coincidentally, when we had just started working on the podcast, we experienced another surprise. Over the Fourth of July weekend, Emily and Abby each received Facebook messages from a young man named Jordan.

I was at our lake house with my parents getting ready for the holiday when Abby FaceTimed me. I immediately noticed that she was upset, and as soon as she began to speak, she started to cry. She blurted out the news and read the message Jordan had sent.

> *Hi. So I know that this is a little strange seeing as you don't know me. Please bear with me here. I promise you it's important.*
>
> *My name is Jordan. I'd like to go ahead and apologize if what I'm about to tell you kinda messes with your head. I know it certainly did mine when I found out.*

So I'm gonna start with a little bit of history here……I was born in 1990 to Yvette in Dayton Ohio. A bastard to a single mother. Focus on the single mother bit. Ya see I was 9 at the point where I really started asking questions about why she was a single parent and where my dad was in all of this. She was honest. She told me it was a short relationship. Only a few months long. She was working at Grandview hospital in Dayton and he was attending a local law school. She actually has an old journal from 89 that mentions him a couple of times.

She explained that before I was born she was actually supposed to meet him at a clinic. They were going to abort…. He just didn't show up that day or any day after. She decided not to go through with it and 9 months later I was born.

I knew that I had a small family. Just me and my mom, and I was so happy with that. I mean on the real, she was the best. But eventually I wanted to know his name. So at the age of 13 she told me without hesitation.

John Meehan.

Yeah I know….Heavy shit, right? …. So I tried to google him as I got a little older around 17 and 18 but had no real luck. So now the year is 2020. I'm working as a cinematographer here locally in Atlanta and as the creative specialist for the federal reserve bank here in Midtown. Mom had been exploring some stuff on ancestry.com, got a wild hair I suppose and decided to look up my biological father.

On the very first day of the year, she sat me down and told me everything. Who it turned out that he was. What had become of him. All the dark shit that surrounded it, that he had passed on August 24th 2016....and that he was survived by his two daughters, Emily and Abigail.

Sooooo.... it's taken me quite a few months to really process all of this......here it goes.........

My name is Jordan, I was born on august 24th 1990 in Dayton Ohio, to Yvette, and I am pretty certain I'm your older half brother.

Even though I had initially thought she was upset, I quickly realized she was actually just feeling very emotional at the news of potentially having a half-brother. We went to his Facebook page together, and my first thought was, "No DNA test needed." He looked so much like John.

Of course, we did confirm through a DNA test that he is John's biological son. And eventually, the girls talked to Jordan over the phone, and he graciously agreed to participate in the podcast. After a little time passed, Abby, Emily, and Emily's husband met him for dinner. He was very clear about not wanting to know anything about John—he hadn't watched the Bravo series that aired on Netflix and didn't care to learn more about who John was. Plus, Jordan works with documentary films, so he wasn't interested in any spin Hollywood put on the story. But we were all glad that he reached out.

Emily, Jordan, and Abby meeting for the first time.

When I started writing this book, I reached out to Jordan again. I wanted to learn more about him and how learning who his biological father was had affected him. I know that learning more about John has changed me, and I wondered if Jordan's experience was similar. I was a bit nervous to talk to Jordan, but he soon put me at ease. He is thoughtful, insightful, and gracious. He has given us so much understanding and the space we needed to process what it meant that John had a biological son we didn't know about for decades. He impressed me so much that I wrote a note to his mother telling her so.

Once I had my own podcast, and more people heard details related to my story, I started receiving more and more invitations for media appearances. I was on *Dr. Phil* and *Dr. Oz*, but I had to turn down *Tamron Hall*—the time commitment was just too much. I was still working full time, and all of these appearances, though I was glad to share my story and help others on major media platforms, just weren't possible. It would have required me to miss too much work.

Before working on the podcast, I wasn't sure what to expect. I didn't really know what I would do to help create the content, and I didn't have a clear picture of what the final result would be. But the hard work of helping the creators connect with people to be interviewed, digitizing notes and documents, and having recorded conversations transcribed kept me moving forward. I soon realized that I could do this. As hard as it had been, as scared as I was, I could tell my story.

I hadn't listened to the tapes I had of John's threats in a long time. His voice had been very traumatizing to me in the past, but since he died, I could listen to it without having a sick, visceral reaction. I had outlasted John. I wasn't afraid anymore.

When the podcast was released, it was exciting to see it begin to trend on Audible. The overall rating was high, and I received a lot of messages from listeners. Many were from outside of the medical profession, and I think they found a lot of the aspects of our work, and how John was able to abuse his position as a nurse anesthetist, particularly shocking.

I also heard from a lot of women who had experienced something similar to my experience with John. Hearing their stories was hard, and sometimes it felt like too much, especially if they were still receiving threats or in the throes of a legal battle. I'd hang up the phone and thank God that my battle with John was over.

CHAPTER 19

MOVING ON

The comeback is always stronger than the setback.

When I married John, I thought we had a great relationship. It wasn't perfect, but I also never expected it to be. I meant my wedding vows—for better or worse. Of course, I was thinking that would mean struggling through financial challenges as a team, arguing over how to raise our kids, or not agreeing on where to spend Christmas. I didn't realize I'd have to choose between my commitment to marriage and the safety of me and my family.

When we got divorced, I went through so many emotions. The shock that John didn't want to save our marriage, the hurt that he had been having affairs, the doubt about whether he had ever loved me, and the confusion surrounding who he really was made those years between when he filed for divorce and when he died almost unbearable. But I survived.

After he died, I continued to learn more about who he was when he was alive and why he did a lot of the terrible things that he did. I also learned that I wasn't alone. There are others all around the world living with people like John in their lives. They don't all have the support network that I had or the access to information that I do. When I realized that, I was filled with a kind of new purpose.

I have had people say to me, "Don't you just want to move on?" And I definitely understand why they'd ask that question. What I tell them is that when you experience something like I did, you can move on to a certain degree, but your life is forever changed. I couldn't just put an experience like this aside. It crept in as my children grew and had experiences where their father was noticeably absent. Emily got married without her biological father to walk her down the aisle. Abby's work every day as a mental health professional wouldn't have happened if I hadn't met her father. I have a new grandbaby who wouldn't exist without my abuser. There are reminders for me at work when I reconcile narcotics usage. And when I feel insecure about myself—because it happens to all of us—I still hear John's voice putting me down. I've learned that there is always healing that can happen through the process, and that's my way of moving on.

People are also often surprised to hear that I don't think John had a negative impact on my life. I never want to give him any of that power. Sometimes, at my age, I'm a little annoyed that John had some of my best years, when I was youthful, energetic, and most desirable. But I always bookend that thought with the fact that I had to go through it to end with the amazing life I have now, and I wouldn't change a thing. I may be a bit more cautious, but I'm also still the kind, patient, and trusting person I always was. That young girl was fine just the way she was. John may have taken more than a decade of my life, but I'm not giving him anything else.

Being at peace with where my life is doesn't mean I haven't changed my thinking at all. I've learned that not everyone has good intentions. I've learned that, unfortunately, most people have a story to tell and that my story is no more or less important than theirs. I've learned that when times get tough, I can rely on my support system and my sense of humor to get me through it all. And I proved that if you come for me or my children, I am a force to be reckoned with, as are most mothers.

I always believed that I was created for more than this literal disaster and I kept telling myself that. I understood that I had to outsmart and outlast John, and I never doubted that I would. It was somewhat embarrassing to let others know the details of what was going on and who John was, but that is where I found my people, my validation, and my strength. I found that people didn't judge me, which was what I was most afraid of. I'm also able to share my experiences with John and what I've learned about drug diversion to educate my colleagues by speaking at anesthesia conferences.

It may have been surprising to a lot of people that in my last letter to John, I forgave him. An interesting article written by Pastor Timothy Nutt about the many types of forgiveness explained it best. He talks about exoneration, forbearance, and release. Exoneration is what most people think of when they are considering the topic of forgiveness. That's wiping the slate clean. Forbearance is different in that it's trusting again but operating with the understanding that verification of information is important. And finally release—that's just what it sounds like. You don't continue to interact with that person, and you stop defining your life by what they did to you.

Sometimes I feel bad about the choices I've made. Was I being punished for the night I met John? What did I do wrong to deserve this? Like many people, I have to remember to stop blaming myself because I was the victim. John was a predator.

I fought a hard fight to keep my girls safe and to make sure they grew up knowing that they were wanted and loved enough by me to compensate for the love they didn't receive from their father. I am so thankful that Augie played a huge role in their development, and I am so proud that they grew into the confident women they are today.

Both Emily and Abby are in the medical/service industry and there is no better place in my opinion to spend your life. Work in service of others is the most rewarding career a person can have. That they have enough inside them to not only love themselves but give of themselves to others is my greatest accomplishment.

Emily is passionate about her career as a labor and delivery nurse. She loves being an advocate for women and their own personal journeys to motherhood. Plus, she is an amazing mother herself. I hope that I played a part in showing her the love of a mother.

Abby chose a profession that suits her perfectly. I nearly cried when she told me she wanted to be an adolescent counselor. She was once the child who needed someone to listen and understand, and now she is that person for so many others.

Even though I don't blame my younger self for any of the chaos that ultimately came from my relationship with John, and I love the life I have today, I do sometimes wish I could give her the same advice I give anyone else who asks what I learned from my years surviving life with John.

Be slow to allow anyone into your personal space.

Some of the values we teach our children can set them up to be targets.

Trust your instincts; they are always right and are there to protect you.

Don't let someone else talk you out of your gut instincts.

Never be afraid to ask for what you want or what you deserve.

Never let anyone have your power by staying in anger and resentment.

Keep fighting.

Newfound friendship with Marianne and Denny Luken.

Me speaking to my anesthesia colleagues about substance use disorder (SUD) and diversion.

Emily's white coat ceremony, the day before I told them John had died.

Abby's graduation with her master's in clinical mental health counseling.

Emily, me, and Abby at Bravo's premiere of the *Dirty John* series.

EPILOGUE

BY ABBY MEEHAN

In August of 2016, I was riding with my mom and Augie on the way to my sister's white coat ceremony. Emily had just gotten into nursing school, and I was so proud of her. A high school junior myself, I was starting to think about college and what my future would hold, and I felt lucky to have women like her and my mom to look to for guidance.

We passed a van parked on the side of the road with the name of a correctional facility emblazoned on the side. I saw a small group of men in orange jumpsuits and a few guards. It made me think of my dad, and I wondered out loud, "Do you think someone will let us know if my dad dies?"

Any parent who heard that from their daughter would be surprised, I'm sure. I hadn't seen my dad in more than a decade, and it had been years since Emily or I had even gotten a message from him, so it would have seemed out of the blue. But the most shocking part was that my dad had died just two days earlier and I didn't know it. My mom just hadn't told us yet, because she wanted to wait until my sister and I were together so that she could tell us at the same time and after my sister was able to celebrate her huge accomplishment.

I know why I thought of my dad when I saw the prisoners on the side of the road. My whole life, I understood that John Meehan, my biological father, had a drug problem, had been really mean to my mom, and had been in and out of prison for a lot of my life.

Even when John was available, no matter how hard I tried, it felt like I just couldn't seem to get him to want to spend time with me. I have a few vivid memories of our time together. They play like old movies in my head. I can remember short clips of people, places, smells, and all of the complex emotions I felt when I was with my dad.

One year, John picked Emily and me up so that we could all celebrate her birthday. He booked a hotel room where we could all hang out and spend time together celebrating Emily's big day. My Aunt Donna was there, too, because he could only have supervised visitation. I remember thinking I had the coolest dad ever for getting a hotel room for the day to celebrate my sister. Little did I know he probably had no place to stay, and if he did, there is no way it was safe for a young kid like me to be in.

I remember having so much fun that day. And I remember wondering what we'd do for my birthday in a few months. Surely I'd have a special day with my dad and sister, too, wouldn't I? But a birthday party for me never happened that year. Like so many things related to John, I was filled with hope, only to be disappointed.

Emily's birthday party with John and Abby at the hotel, where John had a supervised visit.

There was another time when John picked Emily and me up and I was so excited to see him, I couldn't stop talking. From the back seat, I was excitedly telling him a story I was sure would crack him up. I remember part of the story required me to make a funny face—so I did. I was sure it would make him laugh, and all I wanted to do was make him happy.

While I carried on with my story, animatedly sharing what had happened, putting all of my effort into my facial expressions, Emily pointed out, "He can't see your face from the front seat, Abby." She was right, of course, and she was just being an honest big sister, but I was crushed. I can still see his eyes in the rearview mirror, trying—and failing—to keep up with my story. But it was no consolation. I had failed again to make him like me.

I have always wondered why this memory, seemingly so unimportant, has stuck with me for twenty years. I have come to realize that it is not the story that meant something; it was the feeling that meant everything. He was unimpressed. If only I could impress him, if I could show him I was worth sticking around for, then maybe he would stop leaving.

I also remember all of the people who tried to help Emily and me while our parents separated, divorced, and tried to share custody. Time and time again, John disappeared and then reappeared months or years later, often without explanation. And every time he came back, I was so glad to see him. Every time he'd reappear, I thought it was another chance to make him stay.

Of course, there was nothing I could do, and as an adult and mental health counselor, I know that. But as a kid, I just couldn't give up on my dad.

I also know how hard that had to be on my mom and Augie, who took care of me every day. They made sure I felt safe and loved. They're the ones who asked if I did my homework and encouraged me to go out for the lacrosse team in high school. It was my mom and Augie who were honest with me about John, shared the facts that I needed to know, and ultimately supported me as I worked through the very complicated emotions that came with growing up with a mostly absent father, whose love I couldn't seem to earn.

In 2014, John tweeted my sister Emily and asked to talk to her. He attached a photo of just the two of them. I wasn't in the picture. He didn't contact me. My feelings that I was not wanted were reassured.

He said he wanted to give her a gift. He sent her his phone number and asked her to call him. Because Emily was older and understood what type of man John was, she wanted nothing to do with him. She never took the opportunity to reach out to him. I was baffled by this. He chose you. How could you not?

I copied the phone number and took it with me to a slumber party. I gathered around the phone with all of the girls at the party, and we dialed John's number on speakerphone. Despite not recognizing my friend's number, he answered. I panicked and hung up, joining my friends in nervous laughter at our daring endeavor.

That call was the last time I would ever hear his voice.

Sometimes I wonder: If I had known we'd never speak again, would I have handled that call differently? Would I have talked to him—even just to say hello? Would I have asked him where he was and what he was doing? Would I have asked him why he reached out to Emily but didn't reach out to me?

The weekend my mom told us that John died was hard for me for a lot of reasons. There's no good way to break that kind of news and there's no "right" way to react. I cried, and Emily said she was relieved. Then I was upset with Emily for not being more upset. Like so many people feeling big emotions, we were all over the place.

A little while after my mom told us about John's death, I got back into the car and we started for home. Emily had to get back to her life and get ready for school. Augie and my mom had to return to work. Even I had commitments waiting for me—school, lacrosse practice, friends. My dad was gone, but our lives went on.

Soon my mom started hearing from reporters asking questions about John, and she responded to some. Most were respectful and seemed to understand how strange our situation was. She started talking to Chris Goffard more frequently and eventually shared with us that he was planning to do a podcast about John.

In October of 2017, when the podcast came out, I was taking a morning class at a local college, then going to my high school classes in the afternoon, and lacrosse practice after that. When the first episode dropped, I listened to it while I got ready for school. Fresh off what I heard in the episode, I went to class and then eventually to practice, as if it was totally normal to listen to terrible stories about your dad with five million strangers as part of a weekly routine.

As the podcast gained popularity, I started to understand just how many people were hooked on the story. When I was in my college class, no one really knew my name, and I could slip in and out of the classroom without interacting with anyone. But when I got to my high school, I had friends and acquaintances around every corner. I was constantly aware of the fact that now when people saw me, they had heard the *Dirty John* podcast.

After the podcast, *Dateline* aired an episode about John's death. My mom was out of town when it aired, so I watched it with friends. It was surreal to see other friends and people I barely knew posting on social media about watching the episode. They were seeing everything at the same time I was—his second wedding, the footage of where he had been found by police, an interview with the young woman he had tried to kill.

I really wasn't sure how well I was holding things together until my coach asked to talk to me before practice one day. He said he'd been listening to the podcast. My stomach dropped. I was so embarrassed. I didn't want people to look at me differently.

"I just can't believe you're here and playing so well with all that's going on, Abby."

He wanted to offer support, and to my surprise, apparently I was keeping it together pretty well, even though every day felt like more of a struggle than the last.

I survived the podcast launch in high school only to experience the Bravo series *Dirty John* release when I was in college. Again, when I was in a large group, I enjoyed the anonymity. With people who knew my name, I'd catch myself holding my breath, wondering if they were thinking about my dad and, if they were, if they would ask me about him, or wait until I was gone to talk about me.

There were very specific instances where I remember feeling heightened anxiety related to people recognizing my name. When I rushed a sorority, I wondered if anyone recognized my name. And then I wondered if that recognition would hurt or help my chances. The reaction people had to my family's story was unpredictable.

Complete strangers would message me horrible things on Instagram. I remember receiving a message from a random person asking, "Are you crazy like your dad?" with a devil emoji. For the first time, I started to think, *Oh gosh, this could be biological. Am I crazy? Do my peers and friends wonder the same thing?*

Sometimes it felt like I was in a movie myself. I'd walk down the hall and see someone I knew and, after a quick conversation, overhear them say to their friends, "You know that's Dirty John's daughter, right?" It was fame I wasn't interested in as I started college, but it was clear the story wasn't going away.

Emily seemed much more comfortable with our newfound fame, but that fits the dynamic we've always had. When we were together with friends, she carried on conversations with ease. When we met our half-brother for the first time, the two of them did all of the talking. In most cases, I'm so glad when Emily and I are together and she carries conversations for us and not having her with me when the media attention felt like it was everywhere was almost too much to bear.

When my mom decided to do her own podcast, I was excited for her to tell her story. In the *Dirty John* podcast and series, my family had such a minor role. It was a weird feeling to have someone like John be such a huge presence in our lives and yet, when his story was told, we were just a footnote. In *The First Wife*, my mom would be able to talk about the two of them meeting, dating while they were both in college, getting their first real jobs, getting married, and having kids. She and John had such a normal life until they separated, and I wanted people to hear her story.

When I think about the most important moments of my life, John isn't in all of them. His absence isn't even always felt. My mom and Augie provided me with a safe place to grow up, filled with opportunities to grow. But some of those experiences with John did affect me, for better and worse.

Grief is weird. You can experience the five stages: denial, anger, bargaining, depression, acceptance. No one talks about how you can reenter the stages at different phases in your life: when he died, when I got into college, when I graduated college, when I became a mental health counselor. I will grieve the loss of someone who was supposed to love me unconditionally for the rest of my life.

Over time, my understanding of John evolved. When I was little, my mom had no choice but to share facts with me about things he had done and the related consequences, like having to go to prison for months or years at a time. I understood that my dad, a man I'd always love, sometimes did bad things.

When I got older, and the list of bad things that he did got longer, I started to see him differently. I started to understand that John was more than a person who made mistakes and sometimes did bad things. I had to admit that he was simply a bad person.

And even though I had experienced that realization over time, it was still painful to accept that, when he died, he would never be anyone different. On some level, I had been hanging onto the chance that he might one day be a better person.

Something I teach my clients is radical acceptance, and it's a technique I've found incredibly beneficial for myself. Radical acceptance involves accepting reality, focusing on what we can control, and letting go of bitterness. It's understanding your life story and choosing what you are going to do to make the most out of it. I surely won't let John control who I am.

Emily and I were both called to helping professions. My mom and stepdad encouraged us to choose meaningful work but ultimately allowed us to choose our own paths. As a labor and delivery nurse, Emily uses her strength and compassion to help parents through the unexpected twists and turns that come with bringing new life into the world. As an adolescent mental health therapist, I help young people and their families navigate the complexities of everyday life. I like to think that Emily helps you enter the world and I help you take care of yourself throughout your time on this earth. Our dad did so much damage, and we wanted to do the opposite. Every day we want to put good into the world and to try and make up for what he did.

Practicing radical acceptance, I can honestly say that instead of being bitter, I am grateful. I am grateful to have Dirty John as my biological father because this experience has made us a close family. It brought Augie, the best dad ever, into my life. It led me to my career and helped me find myself.

Life's not perfect—we'll struggle with some aspect of this forever. Radical acceptance doesn't mean that there aren't still hard times or that hurtful comments on social media stop bothering me. It doesn't even mean that I don't sometimes wish things were different. It just means we can see the beauty in the life we have.

I'm sorry to disappoint the strangers who sent DMs asking about my life, but I'm not "crazy" like John. I am strong-willed like my sister and an unconditional lover like my stepdad.

And I'm a smart, compassionate survivor, like my mom.

ACKNOWLEDGMENTS

There are so many people who provided support and encouragement, both as I navigated the legal system and as I told my story in this book. To my family, friends, and colleagues, your belief in me fueled every page.

Emily and Abby, you both inspire me every day. I wrote this book for you and because of you. You are the best things in my life and I am so grateful God entrusted you to me.

Augie, your strength and dedication to our family has been amazing. The girls and I are so blessed to have had you in our lives. Your unconditional love through all of this chaos has been the constant that kept us always headed in the right direction.

Mom and Dad, sorry for taking you on this crazy ride, but thank you for your unwavering support.

Karen and Donna, I know how hard this has all been for you, and yet you selflessly gave needed insight about your brother over the years.

Jordan, thank you for being so open to talking about your life, and for being so gracious to Emily, Abby, and me as we have navigated this new chapter of our lives.

Writing this book I was also reminded how many friends stood by my side through the darkest times with John. Jane, you are the definition of a true friend, to me and all of those lucky enough to know you. Mark, Perry, John, and Kevin, you were John's friends and became my allies, my help and support at critical times. Dr. Bob, I credit you with helping to keep me informed and safe during the scariest of days. You've been a lifesaver with your personal and professional guidance.

John and Lois supported me for so long. They have both passed, but I want their family and friends to know just how important they were to me. I miss their friendship every day.

I also met incredible people only because of my long-fought battle with John. Denny, thank you for your tenacity and dedication to protecting me and my family. Julia, thank you for being the badass police officer you are, persisting in the quest to find and hold John accountable. Detective Parker and John Burke, you listened to and believed me when I wasn't sure anyone would. So many members of law enforcement worked to protect us from John, and we are eternally grateful.

Ellen, you stood by me for some of the most stressful interactions with John - when we were in court! You went from trusted professional to dedicated friend, and I could not have done it without you.

Laura, thank you for all you have done to help me understand my situation and all you do everyday fighting to keep women alive.

I'd also like to thank Leah Gordon, friend and colleague, for your encouragement and for introducing me to Amy Jauman, this book's writer. We are both so thankful for the connection.

Amy, I cannot imagine writing this book with anyone but you. You handled me and my story with great love and care. You and I both felt this story was important to write, even though so much of it is painful to share. I am forever grateful to you and everyone who supported us through this process, allowing me to share this story that I hope will help others.

ABOUT THE AUTHORS

Tonia Bales, a nurse anesthetist and mother, endured a tumultuous marriage with John Meehan, which ended in a bitter divorce involving legal battles and restraining orders. After John's death and the success of the *Dirty John* podcast and TV series, Tonia turned her experiences into advocacy. She now speaks at medical conferences and on media platforms about drug diversion, how domestic violence has changed over time, and navigating the legal system. Tonia aims to help others by sharing her journey of survival and resilience.

Amy Jauman is a published author, researcher, and speaker specializing in victim-centered storytelling that fosters empathy, understanding, and meaningful change. In addition to her ghostwriting projects, she has authored a number of textbooks, eBooks, and regularly contributes articles and blog posts to a variety of sources.

Amy has a master's degree in experiential education from Minnesota State University, Mankato, and a doctorate in organization development from the University of St. Thomas, and a graduate certificate in crime analysis from Boston University. She also works with the DNA Doe Project and other local and national organizations supporting crime victims and their communities.